中国能源革命进展报告

（2020）

国务院发展研究中心资源与环境政策研究所　编

石油工业出版社

图书在版编目（CIP）数据

中国能源革命进展报告. 2020 / 国务院发展研究中心资源与环境政策研究所编. —北京：石油工业出版社，2020.10

ISBN 978-7-5183-4290-7

Ⅰ.①中… Ⅱ.①国… Ⅲ.①能源发展－研究报告－中国－2020 Ⅳ.①F426.2

中国版本图书馆CIP数据核字（2020）第205817号

责任编辑：张　贺　常泽军　吴英敏
责任校对：郭京平
封面设计：汤　静

出版发行：石油工业出版社
　　　　　（北京市朝阳区安华里二区1号楼　100011）
网　　址：http://www.petropub.com
编 辑 部：(010) 64523546　图书营销中心：(010) 64523633
经　　销：全国新华书店
印　　刷：北京中石油彩色印刷有限责任公司

2020年10月第1版　2020年10月第1次印刷
787×1092毫米　开本：1/16　印张：8.5
字数：100千字

定　价：100.00元
（如发现印装质量问题，我社图书营销中心负责调换）
版权所有，翻印必究

《中国能源革命进展报告（2020）》编委会

（以下按姓氏笔画排序）

主　　任：
　　隆国强
副 主 任：
　　金之钧　郝　芳　高世楫
委　　员：
　　马君华　王　婕　延　星　杨　晶　杨　雷　张　绚
　　何润民　何春蕾　李继峰　李森圣　陈珊珊　吴鼎文
　　周　鹏　孟凡达　洪　涛　段言志　徐双庆　郭焦锋
顾　　问：
　　于俊崇　马永生　毛景文　多　吉　刘　合　杜祥琬
　　李　阳　邱爱慈　邹才能　张远航　武　强　罗　琦
　　金之钧　周孝信　郝　芳　郝吉明　贺克斌　贾承造
　　高德利　郭旭生　曹耀峰　康红普　韩英铎　谢和平
总协调人：
　　郭焦锋
编写单位：
　　国务院发展研究中心资源与环境政策研究所
支持单位：
　　北京大学能源研究院
　　清华大学能源互联网创新研究院
　　中国石油大学（华东）
　　中国石油西南油气田分公司天然气经济研究所
出版和翻译单位：
　　石油工业出版社有限公司

前　言

2014年6月，习近平主席提出推动能源消费革命、能源供给革命、能源技术革命、能源体制革命和全方位加强国际合作的能源安全新战略思想，深刻揭示了世界能源发展的大趋势、大逻辑，阐明了中国能源发展的内在规律，指明了中国能源发展的方向目标。"四个革命、一个合作"这一能源安全新战略是新时代中国能源领域各行业工作的根本遵循。

"十三五"期间，中国能源革命取得明显进展，对促进中国生态文明建设、推动世界绿色发展产生了重要影响。在能源消费方面，有效控制能源消费总量，着力实施节能减排和化石能源清洁利用，改变粗放型能源消费方式，能源利用效率明显提高，推动产业结构和能源消费结构双优化；在能源供给方面，推动可再生能源和天然气占比逐步提升，煤炭供应比例下降并逐渐向清洁化和环境友好方向转变，能源输配和储备体系建设加快推进，多元能源供给体系初步形成；在能源技术方面，积极推进分布式能源、储能、氢能等新能源技术创新，促使光伏发电、风电、动力电池等技术经济性得到大幅提升，页岩油气、新能源汽车、"互联网＋"智慧能源等能源新业态快速成长，能源产业转型升级取得明显成效；在能源体制方面，不断深化电力体制、油气体制改革，推动建立"管住中间、放开两头"的市场化价格体系和监管体系，积极实施"放管服"改革，法制建设有序推进，现代能源治理体系建设取得长足进步；在国际合作方面，强化与"一带一路"沿线国家的合作，持续增加能源海外投资，积极参与全球能源治理和气候治理，大力推进多边和双边合作，能源多渠道供给格局初步形成。

面对百年未有之大变局对中国能源革命提出的新挑战，特别是面向新型冠状病毒肺炎疫情（以下简称新冠肺炎疫情）后的全球发展态势，要坚持能源消费总量适度增长支持经济社会发展，坚持化石能源消费总量和强度"双控"；加快推动能源绿色转型，增强多轮驱动、多元供应的协同保障能力；集中力量突破技术壁垒，力争早日攻克关键核心技术和关键装备难题；破除一切不适应新时代能源高质量发展要求的体制机制弊端，创造公平竞争环境，让市场更好地发挥配置能源资源的决定性作用；继续加大高水平对外开放力度，切实提高能源安全保障能力，大力提高能源国际合作水平，积极参与并推动全球能源治理体系变革。

为深入贯彻落实习近平主席能源安全新战略，遵循习近平生态文明思想对能源高质量发展的指引，扎实推进能源"四个革命、一个合作"战略部署，国务院发展研究中心资源与环境政策研究所组织业内的一批资深专家学者，对能源安全新战略思想发布以来全国各地、各部门、行业协会、重点企业、科研机构、高等院校等相关机构推动能源革命的实践和探索进行总结，并分析国内外新格局下中国能源发展面临的机遇和挑战，展望未来十年能源革命前景，以期更好地服务于国家绿色发展战略，为国家能源安全保障提供支撑，为中国能源革命向纵深推进助力加油。

目 录

一、"十三五"中国能源革命取得显著成效 ………………………… 1

 （一）扎实推进产业和能源消费结构调整，能源利用效率
   明显提升 …………………………………………………… 1

 （二）扎实推进能源清洁化和低碳化发展，多元化供应体系
   基本形成 …………………………………………………… 4

 （三）扎实推进能源科技和装备创新突破，带动能源及相关
   产业升级 …………………………………………………… 7

 （四）扎实推进能源体制机制改革深化，现代能源治理体系
   初具雏形 …………………………………………………… 10

 （五）扎实推进能源领域国际合作，国家能源安全保障能力
   明显增强 …………………………………………………… 12

二、中国能源革命面临的机遇与挑战 …………………………………… 15

 （一）推动能源消费革命，面临继续深度推进节能减排的
   机遇与挑战 ………………………………………………… 15

 （二）推动能源供给革命，面临加速推进能源结构绿色化的
   机遇与挑战 ………………………………………………… 18

 （三）推动能源技术革命，面临多方联合攻克核心技术的
   机遇与挑战 ………………………………………………… 20

 （四）推动能源体制革命，面临深化电力和油气体制改革的
   机遇与挑战 ………………………………………………… 23

 （五）推动能源国际合作，面临世界能源格局深度调整的
   机遇与挑战 ………………………………………………… 26

三、中国能源革命十年展望（2021—2030） ……………………………… 30
  （一）推进能源消费革命，能源需求低速增长和效率稳步提升，
       新型一体化消费模式开始显现 ……………………………………… 30
  （二）推进能源供给革命，绿色能源进入全面发展新阶段，
       多轮驱动的能源供应体系逐步形成 ………………………………… 33
  （三）推进能源技术革命，科技创新进入加速突破新阶段，
       关键装备和核心技术逐步实现自主 ………………………………… 35
  （四）推进能源体制革命，价格改革进入全面深化新阶段，
       推动能源治理体系基本实现现代化 ………………………………… 38
  （五）推进能源国际合作，全球能源治理进入更加多元新阶段，
       全方位加强国际合作继续深化 ……………………………………… 40

结束语 …………………………………………………………………………… 43

一、"十三五"中国能源革命取得显著成效[1]

能源问题事关国家安全、经济发展全局,也关乎生态环境保护与应对气候变化进程,意义重大,影响深远。面对新的发展要求和国际国内形势,立足于当前中国依然是世界上最大的发展中国家、仍处于社会主义初级阶段的基本国情,坚持保障安全、节约优先、绿色低碳、主动创新的战略导向,高度重视推动能源革命,着力构建清洁低碳、安全高效的能源体系。"十三五"以来中国加快推动能源消费结构调整,减少煤炭消费,稳定油气供应,大幅增加清洁能源比重,持续推进中国"四个革命、一个合作"能源安全新战略,能源革命取得了一系列显著成效。

(一)扎实推进产业和能源消费结构调整,能源利用效率明显提升

1. 能源消费总量得到合理控制,能源消费结构逐步优化

"十三五"制定的能源消费总量和强度双控目标及碳排放强度控制目标,有效推动能源消费低速增长、能源结构优化。2019年,中国能源消费总量达48.6亿吨标准煤,较2015年增加5.3亿吨标准煤,年均增速达2.9%,较"十二五"年均增速下降0.8个百分点;平均能源消费弹性系数为0.44,较"十二五"下降0.05。2019年,煤炭在一次能源消费总量中的占比约为57.7%,比2015年下降6个百分点;石油约占18.9%,较2015年略高0.6个百分点;天然气约占8.1%,提高2.2个百分点;非化石能源约占15.3%,提高3.2个百分点。2019年,中国非化石能源消费量达7.4亿吨标准煤,同比增长12.1%,约占世界非化石能源消费总量的22.7%,位居世界首位。

**清洁能源占比上升、煤炭消费占比下降,能源消费结构调整取得较

---

[1] 2015—2019年中国能源等方面数据来源于国家能源局《能源数据分析手册》,以及国家发展和改革委员会、国家统计局、中国电力企业联合会、中国煤炭工业协会等机构。

大进步。中国着力改变以煤炭为主的能源消费结构，推动煤炭替代战略和"煤改电、煤改气"等政策，推进绿色能源较快发展。2019 年，中国非化石能源消费占比与世界平均水平基本一致，已超过 15.0%；与世界平均煤炭消费占比水平相比，中国从 2015 年占比的 63.7%、高出 36 个百分点逐步降至高约 30 个百分点；石油天然气占比虽然仍低于世界平均水平约 30 个百分点，但中国天然气从 2015 年占比的 5.9%、低于 18 个百分点逐步降至低约 16 个百分点。清洁能源发展和对煤炭替代取得明显的碳减排效果，"十三五"期间每年非化石能源替代煤炭的碳减排量近 7 亿吨二氧化碳，五年累计减排约 35 亿吨二氧化碳。

2. 能源利用效率稳步提升，重点耗能行业节能成效良好

综合能源利用效率逐步提高，重点耗能行业能效不断改进。2019 年，中国单位 GDP 能耗较 2015 年下降 87.1%（以 2015 年价格计算，约为 0.55 吨标准煤/万元），能效实现稳步提升，"十三五"规划目标有望实现。电力领域，2019 年全国 6000 千瓦以上火电机组平均供电标准煤耗为 306.4 克/（千瓦·时），比 2015 年降低 8.6 克/（千瓦·时），年均下降 2.15 克/（千瓦·时），煤电机组效率始终保持世界先进水平；全国电网线损率为 5.93%，比 2015 年下降 0.71 个百分点。重点高耗能领域，主要高耗能产品的能效已接近国际先进水平，2018 年与 2015 年相比，吨钢综合能耗下降 4.2%，机制纸及纸板综合能耗下降 6.2%，烧碱综合能耗下降 2.9%，电石综合能耗下降 2.9%，合成氨综合能耗下降 2.8%，水泥综合能耗下降 3.6%，平板玻璃综合能耗下降 4.8%。交通领域，推广新能源汽车保有量近 500 万辆，实施"国五"机动车排放标准，基本实现与欧美发达国家相同标准。

重点高耗能产业继续淘汰落后产能和化解过剩产能，助力产业能效提升。"十三五"以来，中国继续加大高耗能产业落后产能淘汰工作，有效缓解产业经营困难的同时助力行业能效提升。截至 2018 年，中国炼钢、焦炭、电解铝、水泥、平板玻璃、电石、造纸累计淘汰产能 1.45 亿吨/年、

7600万吨/年、600万吨/年、1.34亿吨/年、3.83亿重量箱/年、972万吨/年和1460万吨/年，分别相当于2018年产能的15.6%、17.3%、16.8%、6%、44%、38%和12.6%。而且，重点行业和重点领域能源回收利用水平进一步提高，余热、余压及放散气等能量回收利用取得一定成效。

3. 节能优先理念日益受到重视，全民节约意识初步树立

中国积极倡导生活方式简约适度，着力推进绿色消费。多部门联合发布《公民生态环境行为规范（试行）》，开展"美丽中国，我是行动者"等主题实践活动，全国各地各行业在推广绿色生活方式的实践中取得一定进展。创建节约型机关，完善节约型公共机构评价标准，制定用水用电用油指标，建立健全定额管理制度，采取财政、税收、政府采购等措施推广节能环保和新能源机动车；各地均把大力发展城市公共交通作为重点，提高公共交通出行比例；创建绿色社区，从社区的规划模式、住宅设计、管理运维等方面入手，采用更多节能低碳新技术和利用信息化平台等工具，打造优美宜居的新型社区；培育绿色家庭，鼓励使用节能电器，合理控制夏季空调和冬季取暖的室内温度，减少无效照明，降低电气设备待机能耗等。

遵循绿色发展理念，积极推动能源领域循环发展。2017年，《循环发展引领行动》发布实施，明确了"十三五"期间循环发展的主要指标，开展资源循环利用示范基地和生态工业园区建设，推进园区循环化改造行动，有效循环型产业体系逐步建立，城市循环发展体系继续完善。开展长江经济带的涉水类园区、京津冀地区的社区类园区、珠三角地区的石化轻工建材等园区的循环化改造。统筹规划了京津冀地区再生资源工业固废、生活垃圾资源化利用和无害化处理设施建设。探索实施"互联网+"资源循环利用的新型商业模式，推动静脉产业加快发展，建设"线上线下融合"的回收网络，建立重点品种的全生命周期追溯机制。

（二）扎实推进能源清洁化和低碳化发展，多元化供应体系基本形成

1. 能源供应多元体系逐步建立，供应布局继续优化

国内多种能源保障能力增强，非化石能源等规模位居世界第一。 中国能源供应保障体系基本完善，能源生产总量、煤炭产量、电力装机规模及发电量均居世界首位。2019年，国内一次能源生产总量达39.7亿吨标准煤，比2015年增加约3.6亿吨，其中煤炭产量为38.5亿吨，原油产量为1.9亿吨，天然气产量为1736亿立方米❶，全口径发电量达7.5万亿千瓦·时（非化石能源发电量占比达31.9%）。截至2019年，全国发电装机规模达20.1亿千瓦，比2015年增加约4.8亿千瓦。2019年，中国进口原油、天然气和煤炭分别为5.1亿吨、1352亿立方米和3.0亿吨。能源进口来源呈现多元化，2019年石油进口来源国达43个，天然气进口来源国达31个。

适应高质量发展空间布局的能源系统基本形成，能源生产供应布局逐渐完善。 一方面，通过一系列能源基地建设，西部地区各类能源资源加强规模化开采和就地转换，完善"西供东用"格局。中国原煤主要产自山西、内蒙古、陕西、新疆四省和自治区，占全国总产量的75%以上；油气主要产地为东北、西北的陕西和新疆、西南的四川和重庆、华东的山东、渤海湾和南海近海海域；水电资源主要分布在四川、云南和贵州等西南地区，核电主要集中在东部沿海地区，内陆风电资源以西北、华北、东北"三北"地区为主。另一方面，东中部能源需求集中地区，加强电力和石油炼制等能源加工转换能力布局，使其更贴近终端能源需求侧，同时积极发展风电、光伏、生物质等分布式能源资源开发利用模式，逐步形成"能从远方来"与"能从身边来"并重格局。

---

❶ 一次能源生产量不含煤制气。

2. 煤炭清洁高效生产利用水平提升，非化石能源较快发展

化解煤炭、煤电等领域过剩产能，推进煤炭清洁高效生产利用。 煤炭产业格局继续完善，集中度进一步提高。2014年至2019年累计退出煤炭落后产能9亿吨，淘汰关停落后煤电机组3000万千瓦以上，建成14个大型煤炭现代化生产基地（产量之和占比达90%）。"十三五"期间，中国煤炭产量虽逐年上升，但至2019年占全国一次能源生产总量比例降至68.6%，较2015年下降3.6个百分点；煤电装机规模小幅增长，截至2019年，装机规模约为10.4亿千瓦，占全国电力总装机容量的比例为51.7%，较2015年下降7.3个百分点。现役煤电机组全面实现脱硫、脱硝，有序关停30万千瓦以下煤电机组，高效超低排放煤电机组占比不断提高（达到85.6%）。

非化石能源实现规模化发展，能源供给结构持续优化。 截至2019年，中国水电、风电、光伏发电装机规模和核电在建规模均居世界首位，非化石能源发电装机容量占中国总装机的42%，可再生能源发电装机规模达7.9亿千瓦，占电力总装机容量的39.5%，其中水电、风电和光伏分别为3.6亿千瓦、2.1亿千瓦和2.0亿千瓦，与2015年相比分别增长12.5%、62.8%和363.2%；核电在运装机规模达4874万千瓦，在建装机规模约为1000万千瓦，2020年9月，国务院核准海南昌江二期、浙江三澳一期工程。2019年，非化石能源在国内能源供给结构中的占比达18.8%，比2015年增加4.3个百分点，其中水电发电量为1.3万亿千瓦·时（占一次能源供给比例达9.5%），风电、光伏发电量分别为4057亿千瓦·时和2243亿千瓦·时，核电发电量为3487亿千瓦·时。"十三五"前四年，国内能源供给增量为5.1亿吨标准煤，其中非化石能源贡献度达50%左右。同时，氢能等新能源较快发展，地热能、生物质能开发利用逐步受到重视。

3. 全国统一的能源基础设施网络基本建成，智慧能源生产体系建设有序推进

能源基础设施建设取得成效，能源调峰储备体系初步建成。 能源运

输能力得到增强，总体有效支撑了能源从西北（晋陕蒙）及西南（川滇）往华北、华中、华东和华南地区，以及从蒙东往东北地区的能源流向。有序推进煤炭运输通道建设，形成"西煤东运、北煤南调"运输网络，截至2019年中国主要煤炭铁路运输里程达2万千米以上，铁路煤炭年发运量达24.6亿吨，占煤炭产量的64%；天然气产供储销体系建设取得进展，"西气东输、北气南下、海气登陆"互联互通格局初步形成，截至2019年天然气干线管道里程超过8.7万千米，一次输气能力超过3500亿立方米/年；原油和成品油管道布局进一步完善，基本形成"西油东送、北油南下、沿海内送"格局，截至2019年原油管道、成品油管道里程分别达到3.0万千米和2.8万千米；12条大气污染防治行动重点输电通道基本建成，总体形成"西电东送"电力输送格局，截至2019年220千伏及以上输电线路长度达75.5万千米，35千伏及以上输电线路长度接近200万千米，西电东送能力约为3亿千瓦。积极构建多层次、多元化调峰储备体系，能源应急保障能力得到提升。截至2019年，累计建成27座地下储气库，有效工作气量达102亿立方米；抽水蓄能电站总装机容量突破3000万千瓦，在建装机容量达5000万千瓦以上；优化石油储备布局和结构，提高石油储备规模，基本完成"十三五"规划目标要求的储备总规模。

推动能源生产与现代信息领域深度融合，智慧能源生产系统建设初见成效。 能源生产与通信领域加速渗透，能源生产智能化系统建设有序推进，"第五代移动通信（5G）技术＋智慧矿山"建设取得一定进展，截至2019年已建成200多处采煤、掘进智能化工作面；主要发电企业积极开展智慧电厂示范工程、样板工程建设；炼化企业智能化水平不断提高，在线检测、在线分析、在线调和、智能化控制等技术推动国内多数炼厂实现自动生产、智能安防应急响应。在油气勘探开发方面，对三维地震勘探、测井、钻井等海量地下数据的不断挖掘和运用，提升页岩油气资源"甜点"的发现成功率，助力川渝页岩气、大港和新疆页岩油勘探取得重大发现；"智慧油田"建设步伐继续加快，截至2019年全国在产油气井、场站数字化覆盖率达90%以上，"无人值守"采油、采气厂站不断增多，布置 6～10 口井的"井工厂"油气开采平台陆续出现，有效增加了油气产能。

（三）扎实推进能源科技和装备创新突破，带动能源及相关产业升级

1. 先进能源开发与高效利用技术不断创新，绿色能源技术实现大规模推广

能源开发、储运及利用技术和装备创新均获得进展，科技水平得到提升。中国能源技术逐步显现从跟随模仿到并行引领的转变，走上洋为中用、自主创新的发展道路。煤炭开采领域，千万吨煤炭综采、智慧矿山技术达国际领先水平；油气开采领域，三次采油和复杂区块油气开发等技术和装备达到世界先进水平，随钻测井、连续油管钻井、高精度三维地震勘探等技术取得较大进步；油气储运领域，长输管道电驱压缩机组等成套设备基本实现自主化，第三代大输量天然气管道工程技术和复杂地表气候条件管道设计、储气库建设技术实现突破；电力生产领域，超超临界火电技术广泛应用，建成全球技术最先进的清洁煤电体系；电能传输领域，1000 千伏特高压交流和 ±800 千伏特高压直流技术及成套设备达到国际领先水平，多端柔性直流配电网关键技术取得突破。

新能源技术不断取得进步，能源清洁利用技术广泛推广应用。可再生能源发电领域，光伏发电电池及组件技术转换效率得到提升，单晶电池平均转换效率已达 22.3%，光伏发电综合成本较 2010 年下降 82%，单晶多晶组件价格降至 1.5 元 / 瓦以内；风电机组单机容量继续增大，陆上风电单机容量达 5 兆瓦等级，海上风电达 10 兆瓦等级，陆上风电综合成本较 2010 年下降 39%，海上风电下降 29%。清洁能源发展与油气替代领域，新能源汽车、液化天然气（LNG）重卡及船舶改造、清洁成品油生产、炼油化工一体化、烯烃原料多元化和高附加值化工产品生产等技术进步明显；新建三代核电机组综合国产化率达到 85%，小堆、快堆、高温气冷

堆等第四代核电技术加快研发与示范应用。煤炭清洁利用领域，燃煤发电机组采用高效烟气脱硫脱硝技术、高效静电除尘技术，大幅降低污染物排放水平。能源循环利用领域，工业余热、余压、余气回收利用和烟气余热回收利用等高效能源利用技术在钢铁、建材、化工、有色、造纸等领域大规模推广应用。

2. 新一代信息技术与能源技术加速融合，推动多能互补智慧能源系统建设步伐加快

互联网技术与能源产业链逐步融合，深度挖掘能源信息数据价值。能源新技术与新一代信息技术不断融合发展，5G、物联网、云计算、大数据、人工智能和区块链等技术逐渐应用于电力、石油、天然气等领域，能源行业智能化水平得到提升。电动汽车能源互联网及运营模式不断创新，充电运营平台新增充电运营监控模块、移动储能业务模块及 SaaS 系统、能源互联互通模块、智能能源管理模块、O2O 业务开发、车网互动模块等功能，完善了充电 APP 功能并建设公共充电桩及私人充电桩，推动充电设施互联互通、强化平台融合互联，实现物理接口、服务信息、交易结算之间的互通，以及充电桩的托管运营；电动汽车聚合运营关键技术、高效储能技术开始应用于智慧家居和智慧社区，集中利用电动汽车充电及放电、储能、家庭用能等大量数据，建立以电动汽车为基础的社区需求侧响应云平台，协助家居能源管理并与电网运行智能化协同，创造动力电池等终端用户侧设施使用价值。

能源与信息产业初现融合，不同能源业态之间的壁垒出现松动。数字化能源和信息技术、多能协同管理平台技术等较快发展，促使煤炭、油气、电力、通信、汽车等不同领域主体之间的"竖井"渐被突破，通信企业开始涉足能源行业，能源企业进军通信领域，行业壁垒逐渐打破，能源企业推进数字化、智慧化能源进程加快，不同产业之间信息初步实现互联互通。产业界层面积极推动共建共商共享理念，凝聚共识，在智慧社区、多站合一、多塔合一、多杆合一、多表合一、四网融合、车网协同等领域开展了创新

技术和新型业态的深入探索。可再生能源发电、天然气、地热等多种能源有效融合，信息与各能源品种的基础设施之间互联互通，能源终端需求与供给实现充分互动等新模式呈现较好推广势头。

3. 突破性技术催生新产业快速成长，新型商业模式和新业态陆续出现

突破性技术推动产业链延伸，成为能源行业创新创造的热点领域。 能源新技术、新材料和先进制造技术融合发展，突破性技术创造能源等相关领域新需求。光伏发电产业链"十三五"以来较快增长，连续多年新增装机世界第一，累计装机超过2亿千瓦，集中式光伏占比近60%，分布式光伏占比近40%，户用光伏超过200万千瓦，占新增分布式光伏的1/3左右。新能源汽车产业链引入自充电销售、自充电租赁、裸车销售电池租赁、充换电兼容等模式，平衡汽车制造企业、电池制造企业、电池运营企业、电力企业、消费者等多方利益，推动上中下游新兴产业较快发展。新能源装备制造及相关产业的相继兴起，使得光伏发电、风电、汽车等新能源装备出口多年增长，促进了相关产业转型升级，形成经济增长新动能。

能源新技术支撑商业模式创新，新模式推动重构新型能源生态圈。 能源互联网新技术不断出现，以及国家级首批55个"互联网+"智慧能源示范项目逐渐落地，有力地支撑了商业模式创新，通过资本、产权、人才等市场提高参与方的积极性，促进能量流、信息流、价值流、资金流等"多流融合"，创建了能源营销电商化、交易金融化、投资市场化等新型商业模式，推动形成致力于为客户提供解决方案的综合能源公司（IEC）。综合能源服务理念及模式打破了不同能源品种单独规划、设计和运行的传统方式，力图做到横向"电热冷气水"多能源品种、纵向"源网荷储"多供应环节之间的协同。通过分布式能源、隔墙售电、需求侧响应等创新技术和商业模式，推动实现"互联网+"能源生产者、消费者、运营者、储运者与监管者的信息融通，由此组成的生态圈改变传统生产端与消费端各自分立局面，提高能源自由交易程度，推动形成新型能源

生态系统，减少能源区域供需失衡和结构性浪费，以提升全社会综合能效，降低企业运营成本。

（四）扎实推进能源体制机制改革深化，现代能源治理体系初具雏形

1. 能源市场垄断局面出现积极变化，有序竞争的市场体系逐步建立

能源体制机制改革不断向深水区迈进，顶层设计和配套政策陆续出台。"十三五"期间，国家相继出台《关于进一步深化电力体制改革的若干意见》《关于深化石油天然气体制改革的若干意见》《关于统筹推进自然资源资产产权制度改革的指导意见》《关于取消和下放一批行政许可事项的决定》等重要改革开放纲领性文件，全面统筹能源领域改革开放，推动全国及各地能源市场、管理与监管体系的建设和完善。以一些大型企业为主体、众多中小企业参与的能源市场结构初步形成，油气等领域上中下游一体化垄断局面逐渐被打破，能源领域国有资本运营公司改革和混合所有制改革不断深化，微观市场主体活力得到增强，推动加快建立统一开放、竞争有序、监管高效的能源市场体系。

电力体制、油气体制改革有序推进，市场化程度得到提升。电力领域改革试点已基本实现全覆盖，形成了综合试点为主、多种模式探索并举的局面。电力交易机构股份制改造有序推进；电力现货市场建设试点部分进入试运行，中长期电力交易机制继续完善，市场化交易电量不断增加，开展分布式发电市场化交易试点；增量配电业务改革试点已进入第六批；电力价格改革力度加大。石油天然气领域改革取得积极进展，全产业链改革整体推进。推动放开油气勘探开发市场，推进矿业权竞争性出让，引入社会资本开展油气勘探开发；组建国家油气管网公司，推动各级各类长输管道、省级管网运输与销售分离和向第三方市场主体公平开放；城镇燃气领域、成品油下游环节进一步放开，鼓励更多市场主体参与，市场结构更趋多元。

2. 能源商品属性开始回归，推动逐步建立由市场决定的价格机制

能源价格市场化改革步伐加快，市场价格体系初步成型。 国家陆续出台《关于推进价格机制改革的若干意见》《关于新时代加快完善社会主义市场经济体制的意见》等重要改革指导性文件。按照"管住中间、放开两头"总体思路，稳步推进电力、石油、天然气、热力等能源价格改革，注重考虑困难群众和特殊机构的价格承受能力，逐步减少交叉补贴，逐渐建立市场化价格形成机制，促进市场主体多元化竞争；继续完善有利于节能减排的价格政策，力图促使能源价格能够真正反映能源资源稀缺程度、环境治理和应对气候变化等外部性成本，通过出台差别电价、气价等多项价格措施和差异化政策，推动能源等相关领域供给侧结构性改革和大气环境污染防治。

竞争性环节陆续放开，已初步形成由市场决定的能源价格机制。 电力领域有序推动放开发用电计划的电力市场化改革，推行大用户与发电企业直接交易，初步形成以中长期合同为主的市场交易方式；可再生能源项目招标制度继续完善，风电和光伏发电向平价、竞价上网阶段过渡。原油价格已实现与国际石油市场接轨，由供需双方参照国际市场价格协商确定；汽柴油批发零售价格仍为政府指导价，但最高限价政策推动价格市场化进程加快。天然气门站价格初步实现由企业自主协商决定，由市场主导形成；居民用气和非居民用气价格基本实现并轨，直供气、化肥用气、储气库天然气价格放开。同时，上海、重庆石油天然气交易中心在国内油气交易产品等方面进行了有益探索。

3. 能源"放管服"工作取得积极进展，监管机制和法制建设稳步推进

能源领域"放管服"改革工作整体有序推进，能源监管得到加强和完善。 行政审批事项取消下放比例超过70%，煤层气矿业权审批及炼化、LNG接收站、加油站等投资建设项目审批权限陆续下放到省级乃至地市级行政主管部门，继续推进电力业务许可办理"最多跑一次"，开展自

贸区"证照分离"全覆盖试点,"获得电力"指标在世界银行排名上升至第 12 位。能源监管体系进一步完善,先后出台创新能源监督管理机制、强化后续监管、核准权限下放后加强规划建设等政策文件,明确事中事后监管的重点任务、监管标准、工作流程和监管措施;积极推进信用监管、"互联网＋监管"建设,"双随机、一公开"监管制度得到完善,并在 85% 以上的市场监管执法事项中有效实施。

能源法制建设稳步推进,依法行政能力得到提升。《能源法（征求意见稿）》公开征求意见,《煤炭法》完成修订,《电力法》《石油天然气管道保护法》修订工作先后启动;国务院发布《关于促进天然气协调稳定发展的若干意见》,多部委联合发布《关于促进非水可再生能源发电健康发展的若干意见》,对清洁能源领域健康可持续发展提供了有效指导。陆续发布《油气管网设施公平开放监管办法》等相关政策,电力、油气管网环节的监管制度和监管机制继续完善。依法行政水平进一步提升,开展《可再生能源法》执法检查,深入开展行业普法工作,建立和完善统一监管机制、协调机制、社会参与机制,项目核准、资金使用、行政处罚等事项决策程序得到规范,畅通行政复议和行政应诉渠道。

（五）扎实推进能源领域国际合作,国家能源安全保障能力明显增强

1. 全球能源治理参与程度加深,多边和双边能源国际合作逐步深入

积极推动全球能源治理进程,国际能源事务话语权得到增强。 参与多边合作机制 30 余项,与国际能源署（IEA）、国际能源论坛（IEF）及国际能源宪章（IEC）等多边机构开展密切合作。正式成为国际能源署联盟国;作为东道国成功举办 G20 能源转型工作组会议及能源部长会;推动成立上合组织能源俱乐部;成功举办中俄能源商务论坛、亚太经济合作组织（APEC）能源部长会、国际能源变革论坛等具有重要影响的国际

性活动；积极参与国际天然气联盟（IGU）的组织管理工作等。参与历年世界经济论坛、柏林能源转型对话、世界能源大会、亚洲能源部长圆桌会议、国际可再生能源大会和"东盟+3"暨东亚峰会能源部长会、金砖国家能源部长会等重要国际多边会议。

广泛开展双边合作，积极参与更加有序、更加包容的全球能源治理架构建设。建立双边合作机制50余项，搭建了中国—欧盟对话机制及中欧能源合作平台、中国—欧佩克高级别能源对话机制，定期召开中巴经济走廊能源工作组会议、中国—瑞士能源工作组会议、中国—瑞典能源工作组会议等。双边能源合作继续推进，积极布局海外能源市场，务实推动与英国、土耳其、保加利亚等国核电合作，积极磋商中沙能源合作，中巴经济走廊及与阿联酋、巴西、伊拉克、缅甸等能源合作取得进展，进一步推动双边能源合作平台建设。

2. 高水平开放格局初步显现，能源进口通道逐步完善

中国实行高水平投资自由化便利化政策，营造更加公平透明、更有吸引力的投资环境。"十三五"以来，面对复杂多变的国际环境，中国坚定践行高水平开放，支持经济全球化和贸易自由化，主动向世界开放市场，先后修订了一系列关于外资准入的政策，由商品和要素流动型开放向规则和标准等制度型开放转变。2016年，开始修订相关外资管理法律，删除原有"外资三法"及台湾同胞投资保护法中涉及投资审批的条款，将负面清单管理模式正式推广到全国。2019年，出台《外商投资法》，从法律层面明确了中国已全面实行准入前国民待遇加负面清单的管理制度，并于2020年正式实施。自2017年起逐年修订的《外商投资准入特别管理措施(负面清单)》放宽能源资源领域准入限制，取消了石油、天然气勘探开发限于合资、合作的限制等相关外资准入政策。

中国能源进口通道不断完善，在开放格局下继续提高能源安全保障水平。能源进口长期坚持通道多元、海陆并举、均衡发展的思路，"十三五"以来，中国西北、东北、西南和海上四大油气进口通道持续推进，陆海内外联动、

东西双向开放格局逐步形成。尤其是 2019 年底中俄东线（北段）天然气管道投运，对东北、华北甚至华东地区形成有力的天然气供应支撑，标志着中国四大进口通道布局基本实现。同时，中美第一阶段贸易协定初步达成，包括 LNG 在内的能源贸易将进一步增强中国天然气进口的多元化水平。

3. 能源国际合作取得成效，积极推进"一带一路"沿线国家共商共建共享

中国与阿盟、东盟、非洲和中东欧国家加强合作，建立了四大区域能源合作中心。中国与阿盟签订了《关于成立中阿清洁能源培训中心的协议》，在北京共同建立中阿清洁能源培训中心，组织光伏、光热、风电、智能电网等方面的培训工作。中国与东盟国家建立了良好的互动合作机制，在清洁能源贸易和投资等方面创造可期的合作潜力。中国与非盟签署了中非盟加强能源合作谅解备忘录，在"一带一路"框架下共同推动非洲基础设施发展规划（PIDA），非盟《2063 年议程》旗舰项目合作取得积极成果。中国已与俄罗斯、蒙古国、缅甸等多个周边国家实现输电线路互联与电力跨境交易，中国、老挝、越南三国四方共同签署了特高压送电谅解备忘录，中国与俄罗斯、土库曼斯坦、哈萨克斯坦、乌兹别克斯坦、缅甸等国实现了油气管道联通等。

"一带一路"能源合作程度不断拓展，与沿线国家建立能源合作伙伴关系。"一带一路"倡议提出七年以来，中国与有关国家、国际和区域组织新建双多边能源合作机制近 40 项，签署能源合作文件 100 余份。重点领域合作全面深化，海外油气合作不断拓展、核电项目"走出去"取得进展，有力促进了沿线国家政策沟通、设施联通、贸易畅通、资金融通、民心相通。建成了五大国际油气合作区，在沿线地区承建了一批水电站、火电站、核电站和电网工程项目，带动中国能源装备、技术、标准和服务等领域"走出去"。尤其是依托自身优势、以相对低成本的新能源和可再生能源技术、产品、装备和服务供应国际市场，有效推动了全球能源转型和"一带一路"沿线国家的绿色发展。

二、中国能源革命面临的机遇与挑战

新冠肺炎疫情后全球政治经济格局深度调整，推动绿色复苏将加快绿色能源发展步伐。从"十四五"开始中国将致力于构建国内国际双循环相互促进的新发展格局、推动实现碳中和目标，使得能源绿色转型变得尤为迫切。国内外环境突变，使中国能源革命面临历史性挑战，同时也迎来历史性发展机遇。新型能源消费方式、新业态等开始涌现，推动能源消费革命继续向前，而能源需求增长总体趋缓，继续深入推进节能减排存在难度加大、不确定性增加等问题；区域协调发展与能源高质量发展预期增强，给推动能源供给革命迎来更多机遇，而能源供给安全压力日趋增大，能源跨区输送与供需协同面临更多挑战；新能源技术与ICT技术深度融合，为能源技术革命带来突破机会，而能源技术仍与绿色发展要求存在差距，关键核心技术面临瓶颈制约；推进国家治理体系和治理能力现代化，推动更深层次改革给能源体制革命增强内在动力，而体制机制改革进入深水区，市场化改革阻力仍然较大；疫情后能源领域绿色化进程加速，为中国加强绿色能源国际合作提供广阔前景，而新冠肺炎疫情后不稳定性风险加剧，能源国际合作困难犹在。

（一）推动能源消费革命，面临继续深度推进节能减排的机遇与挑战

1. 满足能源需求的消费方式不断创新，给高效绿色能源大规模应用带来机遇

能源利用与现代信息技术加速融合，能源消费模式创新有望创造巨大需求空间。新一代信息技术与能源新技术的碰撞与融合，推动以智慧能源网为配送平台、以电子商务为交易平台，融合储能设施、物联网、智能用能设施等硬件，以及碳排放权交易、互联网金融等衍生服务于一体的绿色能源网络快速发展，极大地突破了能源产品和服务获取的空间

限制，能源消费体系中生态承载主体可望发生根本性改变，能源消费新模式陆续涌现；绿色电力、成品油、天然气、热力等终端能源产品与定制化服务的点到点交易、实时配送和线上结算等方式，也会推动形成新型能源供需生态体系，不断创造绿色能源需求；同时通过系统优化可大幅提高能源效率，节约能源的空间巨大。

绿色能源利用新方式大规模推广应用，全社会能源消费升级或能大力拓展能源利用空间。"煤改电、煤改气、煤改热"因地制宜、积极推进，"以电代煤""以气代煤"逐步在热力管网覆盖以外的郊区和农村普及；煤炭清洁利用、提高机动车燃油经济性、地热能综合开发利用、生物质能高效利用等技术逐步突破和应用。工业领域循环经济、燃气锅炉、电窑炉等加快推广；交通领域，新能源汽车快速发展，电气化铁路全面普及，绿色交通、智慧交通加速建设；建筑领域，绿色建筑、建筑光伏储能一体化、智慧社区、智慧家居等聚合运营方式和多能互补的模块化能源互联网体系等陆续兴起，或将持续促进全社会的能源消费转型升级。

2. 能源需求增长由工业向建筑和交通转移，负荷特征更加复杂、区域布局更趋多元

改革开放以来工业部门长期是中国能源消费的主力，而当前伴随着工业化进入中后期，经济高质量发展阶段的终端用能特征正发生显著变化。近年来，工业领域认真落实节约优先方针，积极推进制造业高质量发展，同时提高了工业部门整体用能效率。工业体系向绿色低碳循环发展方向转变，促使工业领域在终端能源需求中的占比稳步下降，建筑和交通领域的用能占比上升且能源消费结构出现优化。终端能源消费主要增量逐渐从工业转向建筑和交通领域，而建筑和交通的用能方式更加多样，负荷特性更趋分散、灵活多变，这些对能源品质、传输配送、时空及时衔接提出更高的要求，高效满足多元化能源需求难度日益增大。

未来城镇化加速、人口围绕更多的中心城市集聚，促使区域能源需求增加，复杂性明显提高。发达国家经验表明，城镇化率达到

30%～70%期间是城镇化快速发展期，2019年，中国城镇常住人口比例为60.6%，今后5～10年中国城镇化水平仍将快速提升。随着经济社会发展空间格局优化，新型城镇化、劳动力转移和基本公共服务均等化等继续推进，将大力促进包容性发展，人口和经济向东部沿海地区集中的同时，还会逐步向各区域中心城市集聚。这或能带来终端用能需求增长、区域布局更加广泛，同时要实现满足多层级、多主体、多元化的能源需求和人人享有清洁、低碳、安全、高效的普遍能源服务需要，也使得未来区域能源布局更加多元，能源需求更为多样、日趋复杂，终端能源需求走势的不确定性增加。

3. 节约能源的消费文化尚待形成，形成有效激励仍需时日

建筑和交通部门逐渐成为终端能源消费主体，多元化用能有待形成满足合理需求的消费文化。 随着人均生活水平的提升，建筑和交通部门耗能占比持续提高。居民生活、公共建筑和商业建筑需要大量的采暖、电器、烹饪、空调等用能服务，主要消耗电力、天然气、煤炭；居民出行和电子商务催生公路、铁路、水路和航空客运及货运的快速发展，主要消耗成品油、电力、天然气等能源。这些消费主体分散、对能源需求品种多样，同时要满足消费者的多元需求，使得按合理需要用能将更加依赖于消费者的自身节约意识，而支持能源合理消费、抑制不合理消费的社会文化氛围尚未形成。

目前居民等虽有一定的节能意识，但围绕节能减排的社会宣传教育还需加强。 部分消费者具有主动购买节能产品、设定适宜的室内采暖或制冷温度等节能行为，但在全社会用能行为上仍有较大改进空间，如照明及家电的浪费性使用、家用热水器一直处于待机状态且频繁开启、食品及包装浪费、偏好中大型或者大排量私家车等行为依然存在，节能绿色替代的消费意识总体上仍模糊不清，尚未形成系统的节约习惯。虽然陆续提升相关居民生活领域产品和服务的节能标准，但在全社会范围内广泛和深入人心的宣传教育仍需强化，推动形成个人、家庭、学校、社区、

办公场所等节约能源的消费意识和消费习惯、"节约能源光荣、浪费能源可耻"的消费风气和文化氛围仍很困难。

（二）推动能源供给革命，面临加速推进能源结构绿色化的机遇与挑战

1. 区域协调发展新战略推动能源供给绿色转型，给绿色能源持续快速发展带来机遇

区域发展战略引领中国发展区域布局，重点区域绿色能源转型具有良好机遇。近年来，中国政府陆续出台了京津冀、长江经济带、粤港澳大湾区、长三角一体化、成渝城市圈、黄河流域生态环境保护与高质量发展等国家发展战略，连同雄安新区、海南自由贸易试验区建设等，构成新时代中国区域发展战略新布局。这些新战略倡导新发展理念，要求高度重视区域生态文明建设和绿色转型发展，将有力促进区域绿色能源供应能力建设，进一步优化能源供给结构。其中，西南、东北和黄河流域等能源资源相对富集区域或将持续提升区域经济发展、产业发展与能源资源开发的协同度；京津冀、长三角、粤港澳等经济较发达区域可望强化本区域的清洁能源供应能力建设，有序部署"能从身边来"重点工程。

各地中心城市和城市群加速建设，给城市区域能源系统朝绿色化、智能化方向发展带来大好机会。京津冀、中原、粤港澳大湾区、长三角、长江中游、成渝等城市群建设有望提速，这些城市群包括不同规模的大、中、小城市，按照经济高质量发展要求规划建设大量的工业区、商业区、住宅小区、公共设施服务区等，其具有截然不同的能源需求及能源负荷特性，必然按高质量发展要求建设清洁、低碳、智慧、高效的城市区域能源系统。具体来讲，先分步建设具有标准功能的城市能源细胞体，以经济性供能为目标确定最小规模和服务半径，做到供需互动和自我平衡，保障城市各功能区内的供用能；再依托物联网和能源互联网技术，陆续集成城市能源细胞体，形成绿色、智能、高效、安全的新型城市能源供应系统，既满足用得起、用得上、用得好、用得稳的现代城市和城市群

能源需要，也给未来城市区域能源绿色发展带来巨大潜力。

2. 能源供给仍以化石能源为主，绿色能源持续快速发展仍面临诸多难题

化石能源一直在能源供应中占据主导地位，化解过剩产能难以完全落实到位。2019 年，化石能源在一次能源生产结构中的占比达 81.2%，虽较 2010 年下降 8.4 个百分点，但供应量不断增加，主导地位几乎没有任何改变，产能过剩近年来一直是化石能源产业的痼疾。尽管 2016—2019 年煤炭去产能合计 9.2 亿吨，但至今仍有 50 亿吨/年左右的煤炭总产能，比有效满足需求的年产量高出 10 亿吨左右；煤电装机已超过 10 亿千瓦，年平均利用小时数在 4300 小时左右，与 5000～5500 小时的煤电机组经济运行要求还有差距；炼油能力已超 9 亿吨/年，大型、超大型项目仍在陆续上马，产能过剩压力不断增大。

非化石能源发展仍存在不少障碍，分布式能源面临可持续发展难题。当前非化石能源发展总体比较顺利，但也存在一些阻碍，"弃水、弃风、弃光"问题虽有改善但仍有不足，水电、核电发展不及预期。水电开发受移民安置、生态环境保护等制约更加严峻，且大部分经济技术条件较好的水电已得到开发，未来发展空间受限；核电受先进核电新机组成本相对较高及因安全所致的公众接受性等因素影响，稳步发展难度增大。随着财政补贴退坡，风电、光伏发电产业整体进入平价时代，分布式能源实现高比例并网的成本不断增加，倒逼加速突破关键技术、进一步降低成本，以及在完善投融资渠道、理顺电价机制、多渠道解决并网消纳等方面的压力日益增大；加上调峰机制极不完善、灵活性电源建设不足和布局不合理，分布式能源发展已跟不上能源高质量发展要求的弊端日益凸显。

3. 区域能源与经济发展不平衡矛盾依然突出，能源运输通道和调峰储备等基础设施建设压力增大

资源富集区域的能源发展与促进经济高质量发展仍不匹配，发达地

区能源与经济长期以来难以协同发展。中国能源资源空间布局不均衡，能源供需逆向分布的资源禀赋与全国经济高质量发展的要求有待协调。传统化石能源富集区域的能源利用仍较粗放，西北、华北、东北等区域部分资源相对富集省份的节能减排和技术创新能力仍然较低，主要依靠高污染高耗能产业带动经济增长的传统发展模式没有根本改变；西南地区虽有丰富的水电、天然气等资源，但并未形成绿色能源上中下游产业集群发展优势；东中部经济较为发达省份能源供应则主要依靠外部输入，特别是天然气、非化石能源供需平衡还存在部分时段紧张现象，与经济发展水平不协调的长期矛盾尚待化解。

能源运输通道建设相对滞后，应急调峰储备能力不足。 煤炭生产进一步向晋陕蒙新集中，"西煤东运、北煤南调"需求规模继续增加，加上多地出台"汽运煤"限令，现有跨区铁路运输压力将在局部时段明显增大。原油管道布局基本完成，但成品油输配的区域性支线管道依然不足；天然气管道整体密度较低，重点区域互联互通难题有待化解。随着长三角等区域电力资源统一配置规模越来越大、可再生能源大规模快速发展，区域内集中式电源与分布式能源发展不协调的矛盾开始显现，给电网整体安全带来压力。能源应急储备体系建设滞后，石油储备规模尚未达到国际能源署建议的90天"基准线"；供气企业、燃气企业和地方政府还未建成分别不低于年供气量10%、5%和3天的储气调峰能力；电力系统调峰能力难以适应可再生能源大规模并网消纳要求，电网整体安全难题亟待研究破解之道。

（三）推动能源技术革命，面临多方联合攻克核心技术的机遇与挑战

1. 5G等现代技术加速融入能源技术领域，给核心装备和技术突破带动产业升级带来机遇

5G核心技术体系面临重要突破，未来关键能源信息装备市场或能出现巨大发展潜力。 5G在传统连接的基础上提供广联接、高带宽、低时延

信息服务，适配各种复杂丰富的行业应用场景，推动能源勘查开采、输配、加工及利用全产业链的智能化改造，可催生 5G 共享基站解决方案、电网智能巡检 AI 解决方案、基于开放边缘计算架构的智能配变终端服务等新型业态。随着 5G 核心技术和关键装备深入研发，以及 5G 技术国际标准和生态系统的逐步构建，能源生产输配利用各环节均将得到进一步优化，可望加速撬动能源领域数字化转型，提升能源生产效率和管理水平，提高装备制造领域的产品附加值，关键能源信息装备制造环节收益或将高于研发与营销服务环节，吸引更多社会资本进入能源高端装备产业，有望大大拓展其未来市场空间。

综合能源一体化解决方案不断推出，新型技术和重大装备创新可望推动能源领域加速变革。以新型能源技术为代表的新一轮能源技术革命正在兴起，新技术、新工艺、新装备及综合能源解决方案陆续出现，在不同应用场景下呈现出很好的发展潜力。综合能源解决方案以智能化能源生产、能量存储、能源输配、能源消费和智慧化管理与服务为主线，力图破除现有技术等方面壁垒，向终端用户提供一揽子高效统筹应对方案。油气、储能、新一代核能、新能源等先进技术，以及造车新势力、充电桩、芯片等领域的颠覆性技术或能涌现，有望改变现有能源的生产方式、消费方式和管理方式，为带动交通、建筑等相关产业升级提供关键装备。

2. 中国绿色能源整体技术水平与国际先进能源技术水平相比仍有差距，创新发展面临核心技术制约

国际绿色能源技术创新步伐加快，中国能源技术在支撑绿色转型方面尚有一定差距。国际绿色能源技术创新进入高度活跃期，以绿色为主要方向的新能源技术正以前所未有的速度加快迭代，主要经济体均把绿色能源技术创新视为新一轮科技革命和能源产业革命的突破口，并成为新冠肺炎疫情后绿色复苏的重要方向。美国非常规油气勘探开发技术率先取得突破后，页岩油气已成为美国实现能源独立的主力资源。碳捕集

利用与封存技术（CCUS）已受到发达国家的高度重视，美日等国纷纷加大研发力度，力争掌握和推广这类应对气候变化的关键技术。相比较而言，中国技术水平与世界能源科技强国仍有不少差距，尤其是深层页岩气开采、高比例可再生能源大规模并网、温室气体减排等领域的核心技术仍需实现全面突破。例如，CCUS技术将二氧化碳资源化，可产生一定的经济效益，具有推广应用意义，但受成本所限在中国实现商业化仍有待解难题。

核心技术制约绿色能源产业转型升级，自主创新取得重大突破仍有一定难度。 电动汽车、动力电池、页岩油气、氢能、储能、核能综合利用等技术和产业在中国具有巨大发展潜力，但核心技术和关键装备及材料均不同程度地依赖进口，从而制约产业大规模快速发展。深层页岩油气、深海油气勘探开发、重型燃气轮机等领域关键技术长期以引进消化吸收为主，燃料电池关键材料、锂电池隔膜及重要设备密封等技术都存在严重的瓶颈。这些技术中国虽已攻关多年，但受限于基础理论、材料生产、精密仪器、高端设备制造及科研体制等方面的不足，短期内依靠自主创新取得全面突破难度很大，而从国外引进先进技术进而消化吸收再创新的模式面临国际政治关系调整、知识产权保护加强、核心技术出口限制、商业合作不畅等诸多新挑战，在较长时间内核心技术仍是影响中国能源技术革命持续深入的重要因素。

3. 多能融合互联面临核心技术思维突破难题，能源新技术的投资效益尚待提高

能源产业发展的传统技术思维突破困难，有效打破不同能源行业间壁垒仍有难度。 在传统发展模式下，能源领域分别形成了以煤炭、石油、天然气、可再生能源等部门为核心的一个个相对独立的子系统和技术体系。如煤—电/热供应系统，集中的"点—线"式供应及配套设备系统经过长期建设，对内不断强化上下游之间的刚性关联，对外又相对独立，久而久之形成了"能源竖井"。"竖井"系统通常设置过高的备用率，

且下游用户基本无选择权，最终不仅导致系统整体效率偏低，使得自下而上的技术和商业模式创新成效不大，还成为能源产业转型升级和结构调整的障碍。计划经济条块分割的传统方式虽已严重不适应"风光水火储一体化"的多能互补能源系统，造成技术转让和交流合作渠道不畅，但大量传统能源系统形成的固化效应还会继续存在。

传统国有能源企业技术创新投资效益不高，能源新技术推广应用的经济、环境和社会效益难以体现。中国能源科技整体水平与能源产业绿色转型升级要求尚有差距，能源产业链、价值链与技术体系融合和协同度不高，严重制约能源新技术的研发及迭代。传统国有企业能源科技研发投资很大，但只考核其研究成果却不考核推广应用效果，造成能源新技术投资的经济效益不明显。中国现役煤电机组经过技术升级改造，新建大型机组普遍采用超超临界等先进发电技术，机组效率提升，超低排放煤电技术和热电联产技术普及率提高，然而区域内大规模机组污染物排放叠加，造成煤电的污染及碳排放总量过高、环境治理与碳中和投资效益不明显。光伏、风电、生物质能等可再生能源技术具有环境污染治理和温室气体减排"双重效益"，但环境外部效益尚未完全内部化。

（四）推动能源体制革命，面临深化电力和油气体制改革的机遇与挑战

1. 治理体系和治理能力现代化建设推动能源体制革命，给基本形成"管住中间、放开两头"能源格局带来机遇

国家治理体系和治理能力现代化建设持续推进，全面推进能源体制革命的理论遵循更加丰富。国家对坚持和完善中国特色社会主义制度、推进国家治理体系和治理能力现代化作出重大决策部署，也迎来了能源领域进一步深化体制改革的历史性机遇。2015年，国家出台的《关于推进价格机制改革的若干意见》，明确提出"推进水、石油、天然气、电力、交通运输等领域价格改革，放开竞争性环节价格，充分发挥市场决定价格作用"；2020年，国家出台的《关于构建更加完善的要素市场化配置

体制机制的意见》和《关于新时代加快完善社会主义市场经济体制的意见》，进一步强化要素市场化配置和社会主要市场经济体制建设等方面的指导，为能源治理体系和治理能力现代化建设指明了方向，也为能源体制继续革命提供了科学指南，有力推动"管住中间、放开两头"能源格局加快创建。

能源体制革命内生需求逐步增强，现代化的能源治理调控体系有望建立。能源体制革命推进能源治理体系和治理能力现代化，加速推动政府职能转变，催生革命内生需求，实现以计划和行政为主的能源监管方式向政府与市场有机结合、市场在资源配置中起决定性作用的监管方式转变。能源监管工作或将摆在更加突出的位置，着力加强监管薄弱环节，积极发挥"互联网+"、大数据等新技术和监管结果向社会公开等新手段，助力能源监管方式方法创新，新型能源监管机制加速创建，能源治理效能不断提升。能源法律法规体系可望进一步健全，立法修法进程加快，各层级和各部门法律法规的协调性、衔接性加强；重点领域和关键环节改革或能取得实质性突破，能源治理体系的"四梁八柱"有望加速建成。

2. 电网环节输配体制改革相对滞后，电力体制改革深水区步履维艰

增量配网改革阻力较大，竞争性售电政策难以有效落地。自 2016 年 11 月以来，增量配电业务改革试点项目国家分六批次批复共计 500 多个，已建设并真正开始运行的不超过 10%，部分企业项目因不达批复要求被取消；在建和在运营项目中，由电网企业控股或合资的占比达 80% 以上，社会资本参与程度较低；增量配网试点项目并网、成立售电公司、客户服务等环节推进工作面临一些现实障碍，试点项目基本处于停滞或亏损状态。在竞争性售电环节，目前电网企业在全国大多数地区成立了所属企业独资的竞争性售电公司，电网公司所属的这些企业与社会资本售电公司不对称竞争矛盾普遍存在。因电网企业同时具有输、配电业务和售电业务，电网企业的售电公司可能与电网企业其他板块存在关联交易，

在竞争性售电业务领域处于优势地位，影响了售电侧市场的公平竞争。

电力现货市场建设滞后，交易机构独立性明显不足。电力现货市场承担着电能价格信号的发现功能，通过发现完整的电力价格信号，以引导市场主体开展中长期电力交易、输电权交易和电力期货交易。目前广东、浙江、四川等省份虽已发布试点方案或者进行电力现货市场建设试点，建立积极、稳妥、开放的电力现货市场，但总体来看电力现货市场的建设目标与发展路径不够清晰，以省为单位的电力现货市场建设易于形成省间壁垒，不利于资源在更大范围的优化配置。目前已组建的电力交易机构多数由电网企业独资或者控股，且成立的市场交易委员会职能不明或作用未能得到应有的发挥，交易机构尚未实现相对独立规范运行。少数省份电力现货市场改革试点经验可复制性不强，推广难度很大。

3. 国家油气管网运行机制尚待建立，油气现代市场体系构建困难不少

管网大规模高效建设难度增大，管道等基础设施统筹调度管理难题待解。新成立的国家油气管网公司面临长期合同等诸多历史遗留问题，难以在短时间内实现资源高效配置。管道占压情况比较严重，受到第三方破坏损伤情况突出，输配环节多、成本高，输配企业投资回收难；管道建设过程中与城乡规划、生态环境保护等敏感区域的矛盾时有发生，管道及储备设施建设任务难度加大，今后能否推动大规模管网等基础设施高效建设有待观察。油气管网运营和调度机制亟待进一步完善，油气保供责任划分尚需明确，与省级管网公司的关系仍需梳理整合；省内管网运销一体化、输配中间环节过多的矛盾依然存在，管输费定价及监管机制亟待健全；城镇燃气管道燃气经营许可证是否特许仍有不少争议，城镇燃气管输业务与销售等业务分离改革还需强化；中国油气供需两地之间的时空错位、管网层级多和主体多大大增加了输配保供的复杂性，仍要大幅提高大范围调度和管理水平。

**中短期内建成公平开放市场体系的难度很大，交易中心有待有效发

挥作用。今后 10 年左右时间内，油气资源探矿权和采矿权仍将集中于主要石油企业，矿业权流转市场有待建立，矿业权退出亟待强化，生产技术服务市场仍需完善；下游市场体系建设还需加强，市场主体培育、市场结构优化、市场交易模式探索等方面还要抓紧实施，区域性现货市场建设尚待推进，成品油和天然气的期货市场亟待研究建立。油气现货交易中心仍处于发展初期，交易服务等配套机制尚未健全；充分竞争的市场环境仍未形成，参与主体少、交易不活跃等弊端还很突出，存在"线下先商议、线上走过场"现象；交易中心产品设计不够丰富，管输容量、储备容量等还没有纳入产品设计范畴，难以全面满足市场的各类交易需求。

（五）推动能源国际合作，面临世界能源格局深度调整的机遇与挑战

1. 应对气候变化推动全球能源转型，给中外绿色能源领域加强合作带来机遇

应对气候变化成为能源绿色转型的重要推动力，全球能源绿色转型或将加速前行。 2020 年，新冠肺炎疫情使国际气候变化谈判进程延迟，但主要经济体已逐步形成绿色复苏共识。当前，各国在疫情防控和经济恢复中艰难前行，全球绿色转型面临较大不确定性；中长期看，在联合国《2030 年可持续发展议程》引领下，应对气候变化全球行动仍将继续推进，能源绿色转型仍是大势所趋并有望加快推进，为能源国际合作带来巨大潜力。在各国政府的积极支持和引导下，绿色能源发展可望成为全球恢复经济的重要抓手。欧盟坚定引领全球气候变化，进一步夯实"2050 净零排放"战略目标，提出"尽力避免过去的错误"（即经济刺激方案导致温室气体排放迅速回升），全力推进经济绿色复苏。

中国坚持优化能源产业结构和生产布局，绿色产业有望成为中外合作最重要领域。 "十四五"期间，中国将保持生态文明建设的战略定力，规划绿色发展目标，进一步优化能源产业结构和生产布局，以 2030 年前

二氧化碳达峰为引领持续推进能源绿色转型；同时，积极促进绿色"一带一路"建设和全球绿色供应链发展，加强绿色产业国际合作，着力推动实现全球尤其是区域绿色繁荣。能源领域将以绿色科技创新为驱动轮，以绿色开发和绿色消费为两翼，以重点地区的清洁低碳、智慧高效能源系统构建为载体，推动形成适应高质量发展的能源绿色生产消费体系。中国推进能源清洁化发展的政策设计、先进技术研发、装备制造能力建设、市场经验等方面可望形成溢出效应，或能有效带动国际绿色能源合作。

2. 新冠肺炎疫情引发世界经济衰退和国际能源格局重构，全球能源市场不稳定性风险加剧带来能源合作更多难题

新冠肺炎疫情加剧全球能源市场矛盾，激发国际能源格局的深度调整。 2020年，新冠肺炎疫情造成世界陷入自20世纪30年代"大萧条"以来最严重的经济衰退，加剧世界石油需求增长疲软，国际石油价格跌幅历史最深并宽幅震荡，危及许多国家的能源安全、经济安全和金融安全。"页岩气革命"极大程度释放了美国的油气资源开发潜力，近年来美国在国际石油市场上的主导权显著增强，其能源独立战略已基本实现，并跻身全球最大的油气生产国和重要的出口国行列，成为世界能源供需失衡的重要新增变量，全球石油供给侧显现出沙特阿拉伯、俄罗斯和美国"三足鼎立"格局。美国不承诺石油减产却成功促成"欧佩克+"的减产协议，未来其在新的能源地缘政治格局中的影响力将进一步提升。在世界经济增长预期不确定和全球能源市场不稳定的背景下，国际能源格局正在出现深度调整，使中国努力争取稳定的能源国际合作面临巨大挑战。

全球能源领域大国新型竞合关系正深度重构，未来全球能源有效治理面临诸多困难。 近年来，地缘战略、大国博弈、军备竞赛等传统安全议题愈发上升为全球事务和国际关系的中心议题，叠加新冠肺炎疫情这一"超级非传统安全"难题，使得国际关系发展的不确定性因素显著增加。全球疫情加速国际主要力量对比重组，导致全球能源治理面临更加复杂的政治环境。能源领域投资贸易便利化的努力受到逆全球化的影响，各国

基于国家安全目标和自由裁量权的投资审查不同程度地加强，实现生产国与消费国利益平衡、确保能源系统安全，以及能源产品流动的不间断、维护全球能源市场稳定、推动全球经济可持续发展与绿色复苏面临前所未有的挑战。中国既是大国新型竞合关系中的重要角色，又肩负着巩固和完善双边多边能源合作机制、积极参与国际机构改革进程等历史重任。但中国在参与全球能源治理的途径、资源、经验、人才储备等方面与现实要求仍有较大差距，有效推动和引领全球能源治理体系变革取得实质性突破还面临较大困难。

3. 能源制度型对外开放政策有待落实，国内疫情防控常态化与经济高质量发展等多重压力增加了高水平开放难度

中国虽已大幅放宽外资准入条件，但由商品和要素流动型开放向规则和标准等制度型开放转变仍任重道远。 近年来中国虽不断提升外商投资环境法治化、国际化、便利化水平和营造良好营商环境，但能源领域对外开放力度和进度相比于其他行业仍比较缓慢，实际效果不及预期。未来十年，世界能源新技术发展加速、转型步伐加快，中国能否确保开放条件下的能源安全、能否引领新一轮绿色能源发展方向，关键在于能否系统性升级与改革开放相关的法律法规，能否调整能源领域的创新政策、产业政策和贸易政策，能否在参与能源全球治理中引导国际规则的变化。中国尚需健全和完善能源领域在负面清单基础上对内对外开放的制度体系，实现积极开放与有效监管并举，还要建立适应高水平开放格局的现代能源监管体系。

国内疫情防控常态化与经济高质量发展等多重压力，使得能源领域高水平开放的难度有增无减。 随着能源领域开放程度进一步提高，统筹好发展与安全，以及在增强自身竞争能力、加强监管能力、提高风险防范能力等方面仍面临很大挑战。面对国内疫情防控常态化与经济高质量发展的多重压力，实现能源高水平开放难度大大增加。一方面，疫情对世界经济的冲击削弱未来能源需求预期，这将明显降低能源企业投资活

动，跨国能源投资决策将更加谨慎，加之世界经济力争实现绿色复苏，传统化石能源投资受到较大影响，这无形中提高了能源国际合作门槛。另一方面，疫情防控隔离措施影响了正常的生产活动，阻碍了正常的国际交流。世界各国疫情的防控已趋于长期性、常态化，能源企业或机构在开展跨国、跨区域经营活动时，还需考虑疫情因素，降低交往强度。

三、中国能源革命十年展望[1]（2021—2030）

中国能源革命不断向纵深挺进，正谱写能源高质量发展新篇章。作为全球最大的能源消费国和生产国，中国同时也在积极推进全球能源绿色转型发展。展望未来，中国能源消费持续升级，新型能源消费模式逐渐形成；能源供给结构与布局更趋合理，应急调峰储备能力大为改善，智慧能源生产系统有序建设；能源技术领域涌现更多自主性创新，带动能源产业转型升级；能源体制革命持续深化，力争还原能源商品属性，构建公平开放、竞争有序的市场体系；能源国际合作围绕共建共商共享结出更多硕果，合作程度进一步加深，全球能源治理体系更加合理，中国在开放条件下国家能源安全得到保障。

（一）推进能源消费革命，能源需求低速增长和效率稳步提升，新型一体化消费模式开始显现

1. 至2030年中国能源消费增速持续放缓，温室气体排放有望在2030年前达峰

中国将有序推动形成"双循环"新发展格局和绿色能源体系，力争实现2030年前碳排放达峰、2060年前达到碳中和目标。 实现新发展格局目标亟须推动中国经济社会的需求和供给两侧同时变革，在需求侧更加强化内需驱动，在供给侧着力补齐重点行业的薄弱环节短板。供需两侧的潜在结构性变化将推动"十四五"能源经济关系呈现新特征，能源生产和消费进入新的发展阶段。综合判断，能源需求继续保持低速增长

---

[1] 2020—2030年中国能源等方面数据，基于国务院发展研究中心资源与环境政策研究所经济—能源—环境系统分析模型得到的预测结果，并综合中国电力企业联合会、中国煤炭工业协会等机构的相关分析结果。国务院发展研究中心资源与环境政策研究所的预测模型，是一个在可计算一般均衡模型（CGE）基础上构建的国家及分省的能源供需平衡与二氧化碳及主要污染物排放预测模型，可根据未来经济高质量发展目标和国际经验等测算中国必需的能源市场需求、二氧化碳和主要污染物排放量。

的总体态势不会改变。预计"十四五"期间，一次能源需求增速平稳小幅下降，年均增速约为2.5%，平均能源消费弹性系数为0.43左右，2025年能源消费总量超过55亿吨标准煤；经过努力，非化石能源和天然气等清洁能源占比合计超过30%；石油需求量约为7.0亿吨，占比近18%，煤炭占比降至50%以下。能源品质不断提升，预计2025年全社会终端能源需求总量在45亿吨标准煤左右，全社会用电量约为9万亿千瓦·时，"十四五"期间年均增速约为3.5%，终端能源电气化率较2020年提高2个百分点。能源效率稳步提高，单位GDP能耗比2020年下降13%左右。

2025年后清洁低碳、智慧高效、经济安全的能源发展方向更加明确，温室气体排放总量逐渐达峰。 预计2025—2030年一次能源需求增速进一步放缓至1%左右，到2030年不超过60亿吨标准煤，煤降、气升、油稳、非化石能源加速发展的需求结构转型路线更加清晰，煤炭需求占比降至40%左右，天然气和非化石能源需求合计占比提高至40%以上，能源利用产生的二氧化碳排放在2025—2030年间达峰值。终端能源需求规模预计在46亿吨标准煤左右，其中工业、交通的终端能源需求有望分别在2030年前后达峰值，包括商业和居民生活耗能在内的建筑用能仍将继续增长。

2. 能源消费持续升级，一体化消费新模式日渐成熟

伴随着能源系统向能源互联网转型发展，工业和交通能源消费模式将从传统的单一服务型向多元服务型转变。 工业领域打破传统能源"竖井"模式，逐步形成灵活的满足整个工业园区各类市场主体的综合能源服务需求，建立向电气化转型升级、能源梯级利用和循环利用的高效模式；交通用能力争实现电动化、网联化、智能化、共享化和绿色化发展，并逐步走向"五化"融合。电动汽车、氢气储能等新型用能方式逐渐增多，能源需求侧管理和响应需求市场开始形成，调峰、调频、调压、备用、余能外售等能源服务市场建设加快推进，更好满足消费者分散、点状等多元化服务需求。虚拟经济与实体经济有机结合，依托能源服务网

络发现和挖掘更高附加价值的商业模式开始普及，更加公平、更有效率、更可持续、更加安全、以人为本的能源消费模式稳步建立。

"电气热冷水一体化"建筑用能服务市场建设有序推进，能源消费定制式服务模式日渐成熟。 具有规模效应的、以市场化手段聚合并集成各类能源消费者和能源消费产品及服务的新消费模式逐步出现，兼具供需互动的终端能源一体化服务业务逐渐壮大。突破传统的点式服务向全方位服务转变，集成业务咨询、规划设计、工程建设、运营维护、终端服务等多个环节，跨界融合发展，创新总承包方式，提供整体解决方案；统筹开发建设建筑用能终端和一体化集成供能基础设施，推动多能协同供应和能源综合梯级利用，满足用户对电、热、冷、气等多种能源的需求；实现不同能源品种的互补协同，提供更加多元灵活的用能选择，全方位满足用户用能需要。

3. 能源消费者逐步向产消者转变，赋予消费者更多的选择权

能源消费者角色出现变化，能源产消者逐渐在市场活跃。 传统化石能源主导的能源系统中，能源生产、加工、储运与消费各环节主体分工明确，消费者在能源体系中作为终端需求用户，角色单一并长期固化。随着分布式光伏、风电、微电网等微能源系统陆续出现，越来越多的企业、公用建筑和家庭等原作为单纯的能源消费者可望成为能源生产者。能源消费者可以自行发电或储能，除满足自身用能需求外，还可在电力市场或综合能源服务市场将余电上网销售供他人使用，逐步探索实现产销用一体化。

能源消费市场环境逐渐成熟，消费者地位从被动接受向主动选择转变。 在电力体制改革、油气体制改革向纵深推进过程中，能源消费者自主选择能源品种的意识逐步增强，能源消费者与供应者的关系开始从单向供需关系向双向互动模式转变。智能表计等智能终端逐渐被广泛采用，能源消费者可更加及时地了解自身用能、分布式可再生电源出力及储能设施充放电情况，依据市场信号和系统运行情况主动调整自身用能行为。

随着分布式储能、电动汽车、需求侧响应等为能源系统提供调峰服务的模式相继成熟，能源消费者可实现灵活切换角色，包括向系统反向输送能量、为电网系统提供调峰等辅助服务，逐渐成为能源系统的主动调节力量。

（二）推进能源供给革命，绿色能源进入全面发展新阶段，多轮驱动的能源供应体系逐步形成

1. 优化能源生产布局和结构，加大力度发展绿色能源

持续推动能源供给侧结构性改革，进一步提高清洁低碳的绿色能源供应规模。 保持能源供应稳步增长，预计到 2030 年国内一次能源生产总量控制在 50 亿吨标准煤左右，天然气和非化石能源供给量有望占能源供应总量的 45% 以上。不断提升油气勘探开发力度，至 2030 年国内原油年产量稳产在 2 亿吨以上，天然气产量在 2800 亿立方米左右。统筹推进大型水电基地建设和小型水电站改造优化，安全高效发展沿海地区核电、小型堆核能综合利用。调整优化开发布局，陆海并进推动风电开发，推进太阳能多元化发展，2030 年风电和光伏发电装机总规模达 10 亿千瓦以上。实施燃煤机组大型化、清洁化，加快淘汰落后煤电机组，提高煤电机组效率，全面完成燃煤电厂超低排放改造，煤电超低排放机组比例达 100%，排放标准世界领先。

结合资源禀赋与经济高质量发展空间布局，优化调整能源供应区域布局。 华东、华南和华中地区重点保障油气、可再生能源和核能供应，优先发展分布式能源，全部消纳本地资源的同时积极调入其他地区富余绿色能源；西北和华北重点保障化石能源和可再生能源供应，建设大型综合能源基地，保障全国能源供需平衡；东北重点保障天然气、可再生能源供应，加快淘汰煤炭落后产能；西南重点保障天然气、水电供应，积极推动四川盆地千亿级天然气生产基地及金沙江等水电基地建设。加快建设海上油气资源战略接续区，稳步推进海洋能综合开发利用。优化炼油产业布局，着力解决华中、西南成品油主要依赖区外调入的矛盾。

在一些有条件的地区试点推广开发利用氢能。

2. 加强能源输配网络和储备设施建设，着力提升能源应急调峰储备能力

加强能源应急储备体系建设，提升能源供应安全保障能力。 加快石油储备体系建设，推进石油储备方式多元化，充分利用国际低油价机遇期提高石油储备规模，到2030年石油储备规模达到90天以上。加大储气库建设力度，加快沿海LNG和城市储气调峰设施建设，建立多层次天然气储备调峰体系，预计到2030年建成650亿立方米储气调峰能力，占天然气消费量比例达到12%以上。加快龙头水电站、大型抽水蓄能电站、天然气调峰电站、电化学储能设施等优质调峰电源建设，预计到2030年抽水蓄能电站装机规模达到1.4亿千瓦左右。提高地方商品煤应急储备，力争到2030年形成煤炭年消费量15%的储备能力。

有序推进能源运输通道建设，大幅提高能源资源配置能力。 完善铁路运煤通道，建设沿海配套港口码头，优化内河水运通道，提高煤炭跨区运输能力，预计2030年煤炭铁路运能达到35亿吨/年左右。加强跨省油气输送干线建设和区域管道互联互通，加快城市间区域成品油管道建设，预计2030年原油、成品油管道总里程分别约为4万千米和5万千米；天然气管道总里程约为18万千米，干线年输气能力超过5000亿立方米，同时推广LNG罐箱多式联运和"点供"等灵活供气方式。进一步完善区域和省级骨干电网，着力提高电网利用效率，预计到2030年跨省输电容量约为5亿千瓦；全面完成农网改造升级，加快边远贫困地区配电网建设，着力提升乡村电力普遍服务水平。

3. 推动能源供应集成优化，加快构建多能互补智慧能源生产系统

促进能源生产与信息技术深度融合，加速推进能源生产领域智能化发展。 着力推进5G、人工智能等在能源生产系统中的规模化应用，大力提升能源生产系统智能化水平。到2030年，煤炭智能开采在国内主要产

煤区大范围应用，"5G+智慧矿山"建设取得重大进展；大力推进智能油气田建设，数字化转型和智能化发展取得重大突破，各油气生产企业全面建成数字化油气田，全国在产油气井、场站数字化覆盖率达到100%；智慧电厂建设取得重大进展，主要发电企业智慧电厂建设占比达60%以上。大力推动风电、光伏发电、微型燃气轮机等分布式能源普及利用，新型小微能源发电形式进一步推广应用，实现最大限度地利用绿色能源。大力发展天然气分布式能源，加大力度推动天然气发电与风力、太阳能发电、生物质发电、储能等新能源深度融合发展。

加快多能协同综合能源网络布局，积极推进能源智能调度系统建设。到2030年，电力营商环境力争达到世界一流水平；油气智能管道和智慧管网建设取得重大成果，全面建成智能化管道，油气资源全面实现智能化、自动化调度。以智能电网为基础，与油气管网、热力管网等多种类型能源网络互联互通，与化学储能、压缩空气储能等多种类型储能单元/电站协同运行，与电动汽车和氢燃料电池汽车等新能源交通网络建立有序充电、车辆入网（V2G）等需求响应，与虚拟电厂（VPP）、能源企业等商业主体创新商业模式，形成多种能源形态协同转化、集中式与分布式能源协调运行的综合能源网络和能源优化配置平台。推进能源智能调度系统建设，整合区域内石油、煤炭、天然气和电力等多种能源资源，推动探索各种能源资源之间的智能调度。

（三）推进能源技术革命，科技创新进入加速突破新阶段，关键装备和核心技术逐步实现自主

1. 强化重大科技专项支撑，加快推动核心技术和关键装备国产化、自主化

调整和优化国家创新体系，以重大科技专项等方式支撑能源领域核心技术突破。科学统筹、集中力量、优化机制、协同攻关，以国家重点攻关计划和重大创新工程聚焦绿色能源战略制高点，着力提升绿色能源技术和产业竞争力。深入推进国家科技重大专项实施，部署启动新的重

大科技项目。按照"成熟一项、启动一项"的原则，分批次有序启动实施，持续攻克"核高基"核心电子器件、高端通用芯片、基础软件技术、动力电池技术、燃料电池关键材料、新型电池电解质、海上风电、可再生能源制氢、油气储层精准改造等关键技术。探讨关键共性技术研发项目在全球公开招标、成果对所有企业开放，激发科技研发市场活力，促进国有企业、民营企业和外资企业共同推动核心技术突破。

实现核心技术国产化和关键装备自主化，发布国产能源技术推广清单。完善核心技术创新风险疏解机制，由国家财政、地方政府、金融机构、国有单位和社会资本等共同建立核心技术创新风险基金，加快推动科技成果应用转化。形成多个重大能源科技专项，按照"应用推广一批、示范试验一批、集中攻关一批"分类推进科技创新，有效解决各科技领域产业链中的断点堵点问题，推进关键装备国产化，将科技优势转化为产业优势。在具备条件的地区和领域，发布推荐能源先进技术目录或清单，政府及国企招标采购同等对待进口技术和装备、国产能源新技术和新装备。加快推进动力电池系统、电力电子核心装备、重型燃气轮机、储能系统、深海油气勘查开采平台等装备与技术的国产化和自主化，助力国产能源技术在更大范围内推广应用。

2. 推进建立中国先进适用标准，尽快建立新一代能源技术标准体系

建立解决重大标准化问题的长效机制，重点领域技术标准和国际化竞争优势取得明显进展。健全科技研发、标准研制和产业应用协同机制，创新标准化组织工作机制，鼓励国际标准化组织在国内设立机构。着力攻克重要技术标准体系构建、核心标准研制、全产业链标准化效能提升等难题，发布实施重要核心标准，推动重大研究成果纳入国家级标准化项目。开展广泛的国际化交流合作，实施国际标准培育试点示范，重点绿色能源技术领域标准国际化竞争优势取得实质性进展。

重点布局和突破绿色能源核心技术标准研制，加速标准的试点示范。

强化绿色能源核心技术标准化布局，聚焦能源互联网标准体系、新能源交通标准体系、柔性直流输配电标准化、LNG加注及LNG罐箱多式联运标准化、综合能源服务及储能标准化等方向，催生一批重大原创科研成果和核心技术标准。加强科技成果的标准化试点示范应用，在能源互联网装备、LNG罐箱"一罐到底"等领域建设标准化试点示范工程，推进技术领域标准体系的循环迭代、完善提升和优化发展，形成可复制可推广的标准化成果和技术成果，为培育能源技术国际竞争优势奠定基础。

3. 创新能源新技术、新模式、新业态，培育能源技术及其关联产业成为带动中国产业升级的新增长点

创新能源技术商业模式，激发微观市场主体技术创新内在动力。依托能源交易平台，实现能源自由交易，推进虚拟能源货币等新型商业模式。鼓励省内省外多元主体参与能源商品交易，推进能源中长期交易、分时交易和辅助服务交易。开展多源数据集成融合与价值挖掘的关键技术研发，构建能源监测、管理、调度信息平台、服务体系和产业体系。建立健全企业主导的能源技术创新机制，完善能源领域中小微企业创业孵化等创新服务体系，激发企业创新内生动力，培育一批具有国际竞争力的能源技术创新领军企业。健全国有能源企业技术创新经营业绩考核制度，加大技术创新在国有能源企业经营业绩考核中的比重。深入实施各级重大人才工程，突出"高精尖缺"导向，打造中国高层次创新型科技人才队伍，形成科研技术团队和研究梯队，引入核心科研人员参股等制度，以有效提升创新创业积极性。

鼓励建设能源交易平台，以多种商业模式带动构建新型能源生态系统。鼓励在经济较为发达的地区根据当地能源产储销特点，构建开放共享的能源生态系统，创造更多的商业模式。例如"园区综合能源运营服务模式"，通过构建综合能源运营服务平台，实现园区能源网络内外部数据集成融合，支持多类市场主体开展综合能源运营服务，实现示范区协同能量管理、新能源和储能灵活接入、需求侧响应、多能源灵活交易

和能源互联网数据共享。又如"产业大数据应用综合模式",推动企业自身电源、配电、售电、用电的智能互联,形成闭环联动运营,构建基于企业能源大数据的智慧能源行业融合应用平台,探索多领域综合数据应用模式。多种商业模式促使开放共享的能源生态更加活跃,更深层次地改变传统能源系统组织与分配方式,将能源技术及其关联产业培育成带动相关产业升级的新动能。

(四)推进能源体制革命,价格改革进入全面深化新阶段,推动能源治理体系基本实现现代化

1. 创建现代能源市场体系,加快全国电力、油气等现货和期货交易平台建设

加快分离自然垄断业务和竞争性业务,构建公平开放、有序竞争的能源市场体系。 支持鼓励更多社会资本进入电力领域,继续深化增量配电业务改革和售电领域改革,加快有序放开发用电计划,推进交易机构独立规范运行;探索建立独立的电力系统运营机构,实施输电网与配电网业务和资产的有效分离,深化电网主辅分离,尽快建立和完善可再生能源、分布式能源系统并网规则和机制。对油气、煤炭等资源矿业权完全采用招投标,通过市场竞争有偿取得,继续强化矿业权退出与出让制度;不断完善油气管网运营机制,持续推进国家油气管网公司平稳运行,加快推动管道运输服务和销售业务的完全分离,实现油气管网设施公平开放。

健全能源流通市场,有序推进全国电力、石油、天然气、二氧化碳排放权等交易系统建设。 着力推进电力中长期市场和辅助服务市场发展,加快深化电力现货交易平台建设,研究完善电力跨区域市场交易机制和规则;加快推动油气、煤炭矿业权流转市场建设,全面推进矿业权公平流转;尽快完善原油期货交易市场,建立成品油、天然气期货交易平台,有序推进全国性和区域性石油、天然气现货市场建设,并逐步实现与国际接轨,吸引更多国内外投资者参与,建立具有一定国际影响力的油气

交易市场；研究建立兼容期货与双边合约、中长期交易和现货交易相结合的能源市场与绿色金融体系。

2. 完善能源市场价格机制，强化财税政策对能源高质量发展的引导作用

全面放开竞争性环节市场价格，形成由市场决定的价格机制。将政府定价范围主要限定在公益性服务和网络型自然垄断环节，科学核定自然垄断环节价格，按照"准许成本+合理利润"的原则，完善电网、油气管网业务的输配成本和成本监审制度。进一步完善电力价格机制，建立独立、基于绩效的激励性输电和配电价格体系，加快建立和完善分时定价的市场机制；全面放开成品油及天然气竞争性环节价格，依托石油天然气交易中心，由供需双方协商或市场竞价形成价格；逐步消除能源交叉补贴，加大力度推动居民电价、气价与非居民电价、气价并轨，建立和完善对生活困难人群的救助机制和部分公益性行业的定向补贴。

充分发挥能源领域财税政策的引导和支持作用，建立和完善具有能源资源导向性、反映生态与环境效益的能源税制。深化财税领域改革，以财税支持政策助力实现区域能源供应的"两种资源"与"两个市场"有机整合、"能从远方来"与"能从身边来"加速融合、集中式与分布式供应系统高效结合。深化资源税改革，完善环境保护税制度；构建系统性强、预期明确的财税优惠政策体系，推动非常规油气勘探开采技术规模化应用，制定深海油气、非常规油气核心技术和关键装备研发的专项补贴政策，支持推动氢能核心技术和关键装备、小型堆核能加热原油开采综合利用技术、旋转导向钻井技术等加快商业化。

3. 强化能源法制与监管体系建设，创建高效能源治理体系

持续深化"放管服"改革，创建高效能源管理与监管体制。继续完善行政审批，规范简化审批程序。建立有效的能源监管体系，推动"政监分离"改革，探索设立独立、统一、专业化的监管机构；创新监管方式，健全以"双随机、一公开"监管为基本手段、以信用监管为基础、

以重点监管为补充的新型监管机制，加快"互联网+"监管等大数据平台建设，用好失信惩戒、舆论监督等重要手段，切实提高监管手段的权威性、实效性。综合运用规划、政策、标准等手段，对行业发展实施宏观管理。根据绿色能源产业发展、科技和设备创新需要，强化国家与地方和专项能源规划的衔接性、统一性、落地性和权威性，尽快建立和完善绿色能源发展政策体系。

能源法治建设稳步前行，创建现代能源法制体系。加快推动《能源法》等立法进程，研究制定《石油天然气法》，尽快修订《矿产资源法》；研究制定《能源监管条例》，制定和完善能源监管规则、规定、方法、程序；针对《对外合作开采陆上石油资源条例》《对外合作开采海洋石油资源条例》和《天然气调度条例》等法规规章，着力推动尽快出台可落地、可操作的相关规定和实施细则，有力促进石油天然气勘探、开发、储运的对内对外开放政策早日落实；逐步建立和完善能源绿色生产和消费的法规、技术规范及标准体系和政策导向，加快制订、修订新型能源技术和装备标准。

（五）推进能源国际合作，全球能源治理进入更加多元新阶段，全方位加强国际合作继续深化

1.深度参与全球能源治理和全球气候治理，注重形成更加务实多元的能源国际合作新局面

加强全方位能源国际合作，助力构建人类命运共同体。秉持负责任大国的历史担当，承载为中国经济高质量发展保驾护航的重托，坚持遵循共商共建共享原则，坚持不同国家不同模式原则，坚持企业主体国际惯例原则，坚持互利共赢效益优先原则，中国将以进一步深入推进全方位能源国际合作为重要抓手，在能源领域促进建立合作共赢的新型国际关系，为建设持久和平、普遍安全、共同繁荣、开放包容、清洁美丽的世界贡献中国力量。中国最近提出，将提高国家自主贡献力度，采取更加有力的政策和措施，二氧化碳排放力争于2030年前达到峰值、努力争取

2060年前实现碳中和。

疫情后全球能源和气候治理进入更加多变的新阶段，中国将更加注重提高参与全球能源和气候治理的能力和质量。新冠肺炎疫情使得全球事务和国际关系的主要议题发生重要变化，各国亟须在当前经济增长和就业目标与未来绿色发展愿景间做出权衡，但大部分发达国家已基本形成绿色复苏共识。长期看，绿色发展更是世界经济发展的主基调和推动力，在世界处于"百年巨变"和"百年大疫"双叠加时期，中国能源革命将助力疫情后全球绿色复苏和应对气候变化。中国将积极参与疫情后国际能源和气候治理体系的调整，畅通官方及民间各层面能源国际交流渠道，推动形成更加公平合理的国际能源和气候治理体系。

2. 全面推动能源领域对外开放，注重实现更高水平的制度型开放

能源领域对外开放将更具全局性、系统性，注重进一步深化制度型开放。在逐步放开部分能源领域对外资准入限制的基础上，未来将继续全面、持续推动能源行业的高水平对外开放，从全局性和系统性角度打造能源国际合作新局面。能源领域将实现更高水平的制度型开放，在开放重点由要素和资本等准入环节向整个生产经营环节拓展。在取消准入限制后，将大力提升监管能力和水平，逐步实现有效监管。进一步扩大外资参与中国能源行业投资建设，着力推动"破"与"立"并举，尽快建立一套清晰、透明、公开的市场准入规则及相关配套政策，并在实践中不断调整完善。借鉴国际经验，进一步完善能源领域外商投资的争端解决机制；转变外资管理体系，建立对外商投资的国家安全审查等相关制度。

能源对外开放与区域开放政策逐步看齐，在不同区域呈现不同特点。近年来国家出台一系列重大区域发展战略和区域对外开放战略，各地区有望充分利用自由贸易试验区、沿边重点开发开放试验区等区域性开放政策优势，大力推动实现本地区能源高水平开放和高质量发展。东部沿

海地区提出自由贸易试验区的油气全产业链开放发展，粤港澳大湾区依托金融发展新高地积极创建深圳天然气交易中心，西部地区借助与中亚油气资源国地缘优势加快搭建油气国际运输通道和多元合作平台等，能源对外开放有望呈现缤纷各异的新区域格局。

3. 加强与"一带一路"沿线国家在新能源和油气等领域的深度合作，注重区域能源国际合作取得新成效

依托于能源基础设施实现互联互通的良好基础，进一步加强在新能源技术和油气等领域的深度合作。 未来有望充分发挥能源基础设施互联互通的良好基础，不断拓宽合作领域、不断提升合作水平、不断创新合作模式，从以传统的油气等化石能源为主进一步向新能源领域合作转变，重点向水电、风电、太阳能发电、核电、氢能等新能源领域全面拓展国际合作，推动以产品出口为主向能源装备、技术、标准、服务"四位一体"的更高层次合作转变。同时，对传统的油气领域，将与"一带一路"沿线国家共同应对国际油气市场投资和合作环境的严峻挑战，有序推进重大标志性合作项目建设，继续加强在高附加值先进炼化领域、深海油气勘探开发和非常规油气领域的国际合作。

区域合作基于对未来全球和区域政治经济格局的把控，着力取得区域能源国际合作新成效。 疫情后国际关系和国际秩序将发生深刻变化，区域经济和能源合作有望上升到更加重要的位置。中国将逐步调整能源国际合作顶层设计，做好战略层面规划方向和目标，实施新时代区域对外合作方略，强化与周边国家的多维度能源合作。"十四五"期间有望实现以区域能源国际合作为主轴，以基础设施建设互联互通、贸易和投资自由化为两翼，以新能源、油气、电动汽车等高新技术产业为突破口的"1+2+3"新一代合作格局，逐步推进与重点区域建设能源国际合作共同体的长远目标，保障开放条件下的国家能源安全。

结束语

2020年新冠肺炎疫情的冲击，给中国能源革命和绿色转型发展提出了新挑战，但中国推动能源领域清洁低碳、智慧高效、经济安全发展的政治决心、基础条件和支撑因素未变，能源行业协调稳定发展的总基调不变。未来一段时间，全球能源供需总体宽松，油气价格低位宽幅震荡，绿色发展更为迫切；国内油气增储上产能力显著增强，可再生能源发展前景更加明朗，能源安全保障能力进一步提升；体制机制改革继续深化，产业政策不断完善；疫情催生并推动的新产业、新模式、新业态的持续涌现，为未来十年能源高质量发展提供了广阔空间。

站在"两个一百年"奋斗目标的历史交汇点，中国将始终坚持推进能源安全新战略的重要任务，抓好国家对能源产业的各项决策部署和"六稳""六保"等政策落实；通过加快能源革命，做好能源经济这篇大文章，以科学的供应满足合理的需求，持续优化区域能源布局，推动形成以国内大循环为主体、国内国际双循环促进的新发展格局。

《中国能源革命进展报告》今后将每两年发布一次，旨在搭建一个持续推进中国能源大转型与探索绿色能源领域健康、稳定、协调、可持续发展的交流沟通平台。在此，我们诚挚地感谢各相关部门、研究机构、高等院校、行业学会、企业、国际机构，以及众多专家的大力支持和帮助。

《中国能源革命进展报告（2020）》编委会成员均是在能源各领域从业多年的专家，见证了能源革命的缘起和发展；编委会顾问均是能源领域的资深科学家、两院院士，参与了能源革命的顶层设计，并在各自专业领域亲力亲为、指导推动。

特别要感谢以下院士在百忙之中对《中国能源革命进展报告（2020）》编写工作的精心指导和无私奉献（按姓氏笔画排序）：

于俊崇　马永生　毛景文　多　吉　刘　合　杜祥琬
李　阳　邱爱慈　邹才能　张远航　武　强　罗　琦
金之钧　周孝信　郝　芳　郝吉明　贺克斌　贾承造
高德利　郭旭生　曹耀峰　康红普　韩英铎　谢和平

感谢以下专家对《中国能源革命进展报告（2020）》提出修改建议，以及在成稿过程中作出的贡献（按姓氏笔画排序）：

王　磊　王金照　王富平　史　丹　史云清　白彦锋　朱兴珊
孙耀唯　李　伟　李映霏　邱建杭　何晋越　邹晓琴　应光伟
张玉清　张建平　张道勇　周　娟　赵　伟　徐　洁　高　芸
高安荣　唐永祥　唐金荣　黄文瑞　梅　琦　康重庆　曾兴球

Progress Report of China Energy Revolution
(2020)

Institute for Resources and Environmental Policies,

Development Research Center of the State Council

Petroleum Industry Press

Progress Report of China Energy Revolution (2020) Editorial Board

(in the order of surname by number of strokes)

Chairpersons:

    LONG Guoqiang

Deputy Chairpersons:

    JIN Zhijun   HAO Fang   GAO Shiji

Committee Members:

    MA Junhua   WANG Jie   YAN Xing   YANG Jing   YANG Lei
    ZHANG Xuan   HE Runmin   HE Chunlei   LI Jifeng   LI Sensheng
    CHEN Shanshan   WU Dingwen   ZHOU Peng   MENG Fanda
    HONG Tao   DUAN Yanzhi   XU Shuangqing   GUO Jiaofeng

Consultants:

    YU Junchong   MA Yongsheng   MAO Jingwen   DUO Ji
    LIU He   DU Xiangwan   LI Yang   QIU Aici   ZOU Caineng
    ZHANG Yuanhang   WU Qiang   LUO Qi   JIN Zhijun
    ZHOU Xiaoxin   HAO Fang   HAO Jiming   HE Kebin
    JIA Chengzao   GAO Deli   GUO Xusheng   CAO Yaofeng
    KANG Hongpu   HAN Yingduo   XIE Heping

Coordinator:

    GUO Jiaofeng

Principal Institutions:

    Institute for Resources and Environmental Policies,
        Development Research Center of the State Council

Supporting Institutions:

    Energy Research Institute, Peking University

Energy Internet Research Institute, Tsinghua University

China University of Petroleum (Huadong)

Natural Gas Economic Research Institute of PetroChina Southwest Oil & Gasfield Company

Publication and Translation:

Petroleum Industry Press

Preface

In June 2014, Chairman Xi Jinping came up with a new strategic thinking of energy security involving pushing through revolution of energy consumption, supply, technology advancement, the energy system, as well as strengthening international all-round cooperation. The new strategic thinking tears the mask of the underlying logic and overall trend of global energy sources development, elucidates the inherent law of China's energy sources development, and points out the direction of development. This new strategy, which is summarized as "Four Revolutions and One Cooperation", could be seen as the guideline to follow for all sectors among China's energy industry in the new era.

Over the course of the "13th Five-Year Plan" period, China's energy revolution has made distinct progress in accelerating China's ecological conservation and promoting green development of the globe. In the aspect of energy consumption, through the revolution total consumption has been effectively controlled, energy conservation and emission reduction, as well as clean utilization of fossil energy has been intensively implemented, extensive form of energy consumption pattern has been mitigated, with energy efficiency being improved evidently, and the structures of the industry and energy consumption have both been optimized. In the aspect of energy supply, share of renewable and natural gas in the energy mix has been increased, share of coal is gradually reduced, transition to clean production and environmentally friendly utilization of coal supply is ongoing, construction of transportation, distribution and storage system is accelerating, a diversified energy supply system is initially established. In the aspect of energy technology, new energy technology such as distributed energy system, energy storage and hydrogen has been actively promoted, which makes photovoltaic and wind power generation, and power battery more economical, new sectors such as shale oil and gas, new energy vehicles and "Internet Plus" smart energy technology grow rapidly, transformation and upgrading of the energy industry has achieved prominent results. In the aspect of energy system governance, reform of electricity and oil&gas industries has been deepened, a market-driven pricing and regulatory system aiming to "control the midstream and open up the upstream and downstream" is under way, the reform of "Delegation, Regulation and Service" delegate power, strengthen regulation and optimize service is actively carried out, legal system construction is forging ahead orderly, great progress has been achieved in building a modern energy governing system. In the aspect of international cooperation, cooperation with countries along "Belt and Road" has been reinforced, overseas energy project investments have been increased, China has become an active participant in global energy governance, multilateral and bilateral cooperation is promoted vigorously, and the variety of energy supply channels has been expanded.

In response to changes unseen in a century, especially to the development tendency of a post-2019 Corona Virus Disease (COVID-19) era, we should insist on the aim of moderate energy consumption growth which is capable of supporting economic growth. We should insist on "double control" of total amount and intensity of fossil energy consumption. We should promote the green and low-carbon transition, enhance the multi-wheel driving, multi-variety collaborative supply capability. We should concentrate on striving to break through technology barriers, and overcome difficulties regarding key and core technologies and equipment. We should get rid of any system and mechanism shortages that disagree with the demand of future development, create a fair competition environment, and let the market exert its influence in allocation of energy resources. We should continue to open-up further to the outside world, and actually enhance our capability of securing energy safety. We should make great efforts to level up in capabilities of international energy cooperation, and actively participate and facilitate changes of global energy governance system.

In order to implement the new strategy of energy security of Chairman XI Jinping, follow the guidelines of ecological conservation and energy high-quality development, and promote the strategic deployment of "Four Revolutions and One Cooperation", Institute for Resources and Environmental Policies, Development Research Center of the State Council gather a large group of experienced and highly-skilled professionals and scholars to summarize achievements and experiences made by various departments, industry association, major enterprises, research institutes, universities and colleges across the country since the publication of the new energy strategy, analyze opportunities and challenges confronted among the energy sector due to domestic and foreign factors, and depict an outlook of China's energy revolution for the next decade, in order to better serve the green development strategy, and provide support to the nation's energy security. Hopefully this work could facilitate the energy revolution going into a further and deeper place.

Contents

1. Remarkable Results of China Energy Revolution during the "13th Five-Year Plan" Period 1

    (1) Adjustments of Industrial Structure and Energy Mix Have Been Made solidly and Energy Efficiency Is Improved remarkably 1

    (2) Clean and Low-carbon Energy System Development Is Promoted and a Diversified Energy Mix Has Been basically Formed 5

    (3) Various Breakthroughs in the Areas of Energy Science and Technology Have Been Achieved, Which Drives Upgrade of Energy and Relative Industries 10

    (4) Pushing forward Reform of Energy System and Relative Mechanisms and a Fledgling Modern Energy Governance System Is Emerging 16

    (5) International Energy Cooperation Is Carried forward and Security for National Energy Safety Is markedly Enhanced 20

2. Opportunities and Challenges of China Energy Revolution 24

    (1) The Energy Consumption Revolution Faces the Opportunity and Challenge to Keep Up Energy Conservation and Emission Reduction ... 25

    (2) To Promote the Revolution of Energy Supply Are Faced with the Opportunity and Challenge of acceleratingly Greening Energy Mix 29

    (3) To Push forward the Revolution of Energy Technology, We Are Faced with the Challenge and Opportunity to Overcome Core Technologies jointly by Multi-party 33

    (4) To Promote the Revolution of the Energy System, We Are Faced with the Opportunities and Challenges to Deepen the Reforms on

  Electricity Power, Oil and Gas Systems 38

 (5) To Promote International Energy Cooperation Faces the Opportunity and Challenge of the Profound Adjustment of World Energy Pattern 43

3. China Energy Revolution Outlook for the Next Decade (2021–2030) 49

 (1) China Will Continue to Promote Energy Consumption Revolution and End-use Energy Demand Is Expected to Increase moderately, with Efficiency to Be Improved steadily, and New Integrated Consumption Pattern Is Going to Emerge 50

 (2) Energy Revolution Is Going to Be further Promoted and Green Energy Development Will Open a New Chapter, and a Multi-drive Energy Supply System Is gradually Forming 54

 (3) Energy Revolution Will Be Promoted and Technology Innovation and Breakthrough Is Opening a New Chapter, and Key Equipment and Core Technology Is Expected to Realize Autonomous gradually 58

 (4) Energy System Revolution Will Be Pushed forward and Price Reform Will Enter into Deepening Area, and Modernization of Energy Regulating System Will Be Promoted and fundamentally Realized ... 63

 (5) International Energy Cooperation Will Be Pushed forward and with International Energy Governance Entering into a More Diversified Phase, Comprehensive Energy Cooperation Will Continue to Be Deepened 67

Concluding Remarks 72

1. Remarkable Results of China Energy Revolution during the "13th Five-Year Plan" Period[1]

Energy issues are of great significance and have profound influences since they are closed related to homeland security as well as economic growth. Facing the new era development demand and the global and domestic situation, based on the fact that by far China is still the largest developing country and in the primary stage of socialism, and following a strategic direction of guaranteeing safety, preferring conservation, green and low-carbon, and initiating innovation, the Chinese government pays heavy attention on promoting energy revolution and building a clean, low carbon, safe and efficient energy system. Over the course of the "13th Five-Year Plan", China has been accelerating adjustment of energy consumption structure, reducing coal consumption, stabilizing oil and gas supply, substantially increasing clean energy in the mix. The new energy security strategy, also known as "Four Revolutions and One Cooperation" has been promoted persistently, and consequently there are some major achievements stemming from the revolution.

(1) Adjustments of Industrial Structure and Energy Mix Have Been Made solidly and Energy Efficiency Is Improved remarkably

① Energy Consumption Is under Appropriate Control and Energy Mix Is gradually Improved

The controlling target set by the "13th Five-Year Plan"—"double control" of total energy consumption and consumption intensity, as well

---

[1] Data from 2015 to 2019 on China energy and others are derived from the *Energy Data Analysis Manual* of the National Energy Administration, National Development and Reform Commission, National Bureau of Statistics, China Electricity Council, China Coal Industry Association and other institutions.

as controlling for carbon emission intensity—effectively makes energy consumption growth rise at a moderate pace, and facilitates the improvement of energy structure. China's energy consumption reaches 4.86 billion tons standard coal in 2019, increasing 0.53 billion tons standard coal comparing to 2015, representing a 2.9% increasing rate per annum, and a 0.8 percentage points drop than the "12th Five-Year Plan". The elasticity coefficient of energy consumption is 0.44, falling 0.05 than that of the "12th Five-Year Plan". Among the mix, the share of coal consumption is 57.7%, 6 percentage points lower than 2015, oil consumption 18.9%, slightly higher (0.6 percentage points) than 2015, natural gas consumption 8.1%, increasing 2.2 percentage points, non-fossil fuels 15.3%, increasing 3.2%. China's non-fossil fuels consumption in 2019 reaches 740 million tons standard coal (year-on-year growth 12.1%), which represents 22.7% of the world's total non-fossil consumption, and is the highest among countries globally.

Share of clean energy goes up, and coal consumption falls. The consumption structure reshaping is making considerable advances. China determines to restructure and reshape its energy consumption structure, and promote the coal substitution strategy, the "coal to electricity, coal to gas heating reform" policy, as well as the acceleration of development of green energy carriers. In 2019, China's non-fossil consumption share is more than 15%, which is in line with world's average level. The coal consumption share is 63.7% in 2015, which falls from 36 percentage points higher than the world's average level to 30 percentage points higher in 2019. Oil and natural gas consumption share is around 30 percentage points lower than the world's average level, however, the absolute share of natural gas is 5.9% in 2015, which increases from 18 percentage points lower than the world's average level to 16 percentage points lower than the world's average level. Growing replacement of coal by clean energy has gained pronounced carbon reduction effect. During the "13th Five-Year Plan" period, carbon reduction from use of non-fossil fuels is close to 700 million tons of carbon dioxide, total carbon reduction in five years adds up to 3.5 billion tons carbon dioxide.

② Energy Efficiency Increased steadily and Conservation Effects from Major Energy-intensive Industries Are Satisfactory

Comprehensive energy efficiency has been increasing gradually. Efficiency of major energy-intensive industries has been improving constantly. China's energy used per unit of GDP in 2019 falls by 87.1% (on a 2015 purchasing power parity basis, 0.55 tons standard coalper 10,000 CNY). The efficiency has been increased steadily. Target set by the "13th Five-Year Plan" is hopefully to be achieved. In the power sector, average coal consumption rate for coal-fired power unit of 6,000 kilowatt-hours and above is 306.4 grams per kilowatt-hour, an 8.6 grams per kilowatt-hour fall than 2015, which represents a reduction of 2.15 grams per kilowatt-hour per annum. The efficiency of coal-fired power unit is keeping in a world class level. The loss rate of national grid is 5.93%, falling 0.71 percentage points than 2015. Efficiency of major energy-intensive sectors and products is approaching the world class level. Comparing efficiencies in 2018 to 2015, energy consumption per ton of crude steel falls by 4.2%, machine-made paper and paperboard falls by 6.2%, caustic soda falls by 2.9%, calcium carbide falls by 2.9%, synthetic ammonia falls by 2.8%, concrete falls by 3.6%, plate glass falls by 4.8%. In transport sector, number of new energy vehicles owned is reaching 5 million, CHINA 5 emission standard for motor vehicles is implemented, which is broadly consistent with standards adopted by developed countries in EU and Americas.

Shutting down and phasing out excessive capacity continue to be promoted in the energy-intensive industries, which facilitate efficiency improvement effectively. During the "13th Five-Year Plan" period, China continues to push forward excessive capacity phase-out of the energy-intensive industry by mitigating industrial operating difficulties as well as promoting improvement of energy efficiency. By 2018, phasing-out capacity among sectors of steel making, coke, aluminum, concrete, plate glass, calcium carbide and paper has been 145 million tons per year, 76 million tons per year, 6 million tons per year, 134 million tons per year, 383 million tons per year, 9.72 million tons per year, 14.6 million tons per year, respectively, which represent 15.6%, 17.3%, 16.8%, 6%, 44%, 38%, and 12.6% share in 2018 annual capacity respectively. Also, the level of recycle and reuse of energy in key industries and sectors has been increasing further, recycle and reuse of residual heat and pressure, as well as emission of ambient gas have been making certain effect.

③ Concept of Energy Conservation Has Received Increasing Appreciation and National awareness of Energy Conservation has Been Nurtured preliminarily

China has been advocating simplified lifestyle and making efforts to promote green consumption. Government enacts *Citizens' Code of Conduct for Ecological Conservation*, and launches thematic practice activities of "For a Beautiful China, I'm taking actions". Various industries and sectors have been made certain progress by practicing the green lifestyle—Building a conservation-minded government, improving evaluation standards of conservation-minded public institutions; setting up standards for utility of water, electricity and fuels; establishing a quota management system; adopting measures of financial, taxation, government procurement, etc, to promote new energy motor vehicles; vigorously developing public transportation has become major tasks of local governments; establishing "green communities" from planning, residence design, to management, operating and maintenance, adopting more high efficiency, low-carbon emerging technologies, and using IT platforms and tools to create a beautiful and livable community; nurturing green family, encouraging the use of efficient electrical appliances, appropriately set the upper limit of indoor cooling and heating temperatures, reducing wasted illumination, as well as electrical appliances standby consumptions.

The green development idea has been followed. Circular development in the energy sector is actively promoted. *Circular Development Trend-setting Action* was launched in 2017, which clearly defined major indicators of circular development during the "13th Five-Year Plan" period-constructing experimental circular Eco-industrial complex, promoting circular restructure of the complex, establishing effective circular industrial system, and continuing improvement of urban circular development. Circular transformation has been conducted for chemical and light industrial complex along the Yangtze River Economic Belt, community complex in the Beijing-Tianjin-Hebei region, and petrochemical, light industry and building material manufacturing complex, planning systematically for construction of circular utilizing treatment facilities of industrial solid waste and municipal solid waste. New business model has been explored and implemented in area of Internet Plus resource circular utilization, the venous industry is under accelerating development, recycling network to combine online and offline has been built, and the full lifecycle tracing mechanism for key products has been set up.

(2) Clean and Low-carbon Energy System Development Is Promoted and a Diversified Energy Mix Has Been basically Formed

① A Diversified Energy Mix Has Been gradually Formed and the Supply Mix Is further Improved

Capability of securing energy safety is enhanced. Scale of non-fossil energy supply ranks 1st in the world. Energy supply securing system in China is basic complete. Total energy production, coal production, installed electricity capacity and power generation all ranks first in the world. Primary energy production of China in 2019 reached 3.97 billion tons of standard coal, 0.36 billion tons more than 2015, 3.85 billion tons among which are coal production, 0.19 billion tons are oil production, total natural gas production is 1.736 billion cubic meters[1], full scale power generation reaches 7.5 trillion kilowatt-hours (among which non-fossil power generation share reaches 31.9%). By 2019, national installed power generation capacity approaches 2.01 billion kilowatt-hours, increasing 0.48 billion kilowatt-hours than 2015. In 2019, import volume of crude oil, natural gas and coal is 0.51 billion tons, 135.2 billion cubic meters and 0.3 billion tons respectively. Import sources of energy appears to be diversified, in 2019, China imports oil from 43 countries, and natural gas from 31 countries.

Energy supply system adapted to special layout of high-quality development is basically formed. Energy production and supply layout becomes more complete. First, through construction of a series of energy bases, various energy and resources realize large-scale extraction and localized transformation, the "supply from the West, use in the East" pattern has been refined-raw coal production in China is mainly from provinces of Shanxi, Inner Mongolia, Shaanxi and Xinjiang, the production from which four provinces takes 75% of the national total production; main producing areas of oil and gas located in the Northeast, Northwest, Shaanxi, Xinjiang, Sichuan and Chongqing in the Southwest, Shandong province in Eastern China, Bohai Gulf and coastal area in the South China Sea; main hydroelectric resources distributed among Sichuan, Yunnan, Guizhou provinces in the Southwestern region; main nuclear power generation concentrated in the eastern coastal area; inland wind power resources mainly located in "Three North Areas" of

---

[1] Primary energy production does not contain "coal to gas".

Northwestern, eastern and northeastern regions. On the other hand, energy demand concentrated in the Eastern and Central regions. Reinforcing building processing and conversion capacity of power and oil refining to make it more localized to the end users, as well as developing distributed energy systems of wind, solar and biomass could make a gradual progress towards an energy structure among which "distant supply" is of equal importance with "localized supply".

② Level of Clean and High Efficiency Production and Utility of Coal Has Been Improved and Non-fossil Energy Has Been Developed rapidly

Problems of excessive capacity in the coal and coal-fired power generation sectors are resolved. Clean and high-efficiency coal production and utility are promoted. Industrial pattern of coal sector has been continually improved. The industrial concentration is further enhanced. From 2014 to 2019, outdated capacity shutdown has been totaled 900 million tons, coal-fired unit capacity phase-out has been more than 30 gigawatts, and fourteen modern coal production bases have been constructed. During the "13th Five-Year Plan" period, although the coal production is rising annually, the share of coal among primary energy production has been declined to 68.6%, realized 3.6 percentage points decrease than 2015. Installed coal-fired power generating capacity experienced moderate increase, and reaches 1.04 billion kilowatts by 2019, representing 51.7% share of total power generation capacity nationwide, a fall of 7.3 percentage points than 2015. Existing coal-fired power generating units have completely realized desulfurization and denitrification. Coal-fired power generation unit of 0.3 million kilowatts or lower has been shut down orderly, proportion of high-efficiency and low-carbon emission coal-fired unit is constantly growing (and has been reached 85.6%).

Large-scale non-fossil projects are under development, energy mix has been improved continuously. By 2019, capacities of installed power generating unit of hydro, wind and solar are all ranked first in the world. Non-fossil power generating capacity takes a share of 42% of China's total installed capacity, renewable energy power generating capacity reached 790 gigawatts, representing a share of 39.5% among total power generating capacity nationwide, among which capacity of hydro, wind and solar is 360 gigawatts, 210 gigawatts and 200 gigawatts respectively, increasing 12.5%, 62.8% and 363.2% comparing to 2015. Nuclear power generating capacity is 48.74 gigawatts, power capacity under construction is around 10 gigawatts, with projects of Changjiang phase II in Hainan and San'ao phase I in Zhejiang being approved in September 2020.In 2019, non-fossil fuels account for 18.8% share of the energy mix, increasing 4.3% than 2015, among which hydroelectric capacity is 1.3 trillion kilowatts (account for 9.5% of primary energy), wind and solar power generation is 405.7 billion kilowatts and 224.3 billion kilowatts respectively, nuclear capacity is 348.7 billion kilowatts. Over the first four years of the "13th Five-Year Plan", increment of domestic energy supply reaches 510 million tons of standard coal, among which contribution of non-fossil fuels accounts for around 50%. Meanwhile, new energies like hydrogen have enjoyed rapid development, and development and utility of geothermal and biomass has received additional attention.

③ A Nationwide Infrastructure Network Has Been basically Built Up and Construction of Smart Energy Production System Has Been Promoted orderly

Apparent achievements have been made in aspect of infrastructure network construction. A peaking load regulation storage system has been fundamentally built. Energy transportation capability is improved, which effectively support energy supply to be transported from the Northwest

(Provinces of Shanxi, Shaanxi and Inner Mongolia) and the Southwest (Provinces of Sichuan and Yunnan) to the North, Eastern, Central, and South China, as well as from east Inner Mongolia to the Northeastern region. Construction of channels of coal transportation is carried forward orderly, a network of "From the West to the East, the North to the South" has been fundamentally formed. Lengths of coal transport railway surpass 20,000 kilometres, annual transport volume by railway is 2.46 billion tons, accounting for 64% of the total production. Material progress has been made regarding natural gas production, supply, storage and marketing system, a nationwide interconnected network supporting "From the West to the East, from the North to the South, from the Costal to the Inland" has been established. By 2019, lengths of gas trunk lines are over 87,000 kilometres, primary gas transport capacity is over 3.5 trillion cubic meters per annum. Network of crude and products pipelines is further improved, which could basically support supply to be transported "From the West to the East, from the North to the South, and from the Coastal to the Inland". By 2019, lengths of crude and products pipelines have reached 30,000 kilometres and 28,000 kilometres respectively. 12 key power lines for air pollution prevention are built, supporting electricity to be transmitted "From the West to the East". By 2019, length of power lines of 220 kilovolts and above is 755,000 kilometres, 35 kilovolts and above is almost 2 million kilometers, capacity of transporting from the West to the East is around 300 gigawatts. A multilevel and diversified peak-load regulation storage system has been constructed. The contingent support capability is enhanced. By 2019, 27 underground gas storages have been built up, with effective capacity of 10.2 billion cubic meters. Gross installed capacity of pumped storage power station is over 30 gigawatts, installed capacity under construction is over 50 gigawatts. Structure and layout of oil storage is improved, capacity of storage is enlarged, which basically meet the target set by the "13th Five-Year Plan".

Deep integration of energy production and modern information technology is promoted. Smart energy system construction has made preliminary achievements. Interpenetration between energy producing system and information technology is accelerating. "The Fifth Generation Wireless (5G) plus smart mine" construction has made certain progress. By 2019, more than 200 mining and excavating smart working faces has been built. Main power generation enterprises actively carried forward constructions of smart power plants and model projects. Level of intelligence of oil refining enterprises is constantly increased. Technologies such as online testing, online analysis, online reconciliation and intelligent control have facilitate the realization of automatic production and intelligent security emergency response for most of the domestic refineries. In the aspect of oil and gas exploration and production, constant excavating and utilization of massive subsurface data-3D seismic data, well logging data and drilling data-improved successful rate of oil and gas "sweet spot" discoveries, which facilitate major discoveries of Sichuan-Chongqing shale gas, Dagang and Xinjiang shale oil. Construction of "smart oil field" is accelerating. By 2019, digital coverage of producing wells and stations is over 90%. Number of "unattended" oil and gas producing plant is constantly increasing. "Well factory" pads with 6-10 wells have been emerging successively, which effectively increase oil and gas production.

(3) Various Breakthroughs in the Areas of Energy Science and Technology Have Been Achieved, Which Drives Upgrade of Energy and Relative Industries

① Innovations of Advanced Technologies in Energy Development and Efficiency Improvement Have Been constantly Made and Widespread Use of Green Technology Has Been Realized

Innovations of technologies and equipment in energy development,

transport, storage and utilization have made various progress, advancement of energy science and technology is enhanced apparently. Energy technology of China is going through a conversion from following to leading by independent innovation. In coal mining, technologies regarding comprehensive mechanized mining, smart mining have been advanced globally. In oil and gas development, technologies and equipment relative to tertiary recovery and oil and gas development under complicated situation is in a leading position. Technologies of Logging While Drilling (LWD), Coiled Tubing Drilling (CTD), high accuracy 3D seismic have made massive progress. In areas of oil and gas transportation and storage, large equipment like compressor unit of LNG and long-distance pipeline could almost be manufactured domestically. Large capacity gas pipeline engineering design technologies of pipe-laying on complex topography and under complicated weather conditions, and gas storage construction technologies have made breakthroughs. In power generation, supercritical thermal power technology has been used widespread. Construction of the most technological advanced clean coal power system has been completed. In power transmission, technologies of 1,000 kilovolts ultra high voltage alternating current and ±800 kilovolts ultra high voltage direct current complete set of equipment approached world class level. Key technologies of multi-terminal flexible direct current distribution network have made breakthroughs.

New Energy technologies are gradually making progress. Active promotion has been widely exerted on technologies of clean energy utilization. In the area of power generation by renewable, conversion efficiency of power generation by solar cells and modules is increased continuously. Average conversion rate of Monocrystalline cell reaches 22.3%. Comprehensive cost falls 82% relative to 2010. Prices of monocrystalline and polycrystalline components fall to 1.5 CNY per watt or lower. Capacity of wind power generation units increases constantly, for which capacity of onshore units reach 5 megawatts, offshore units reach 10 megawatts. Comprehensive cost of onshore wind power is 39% lower than 2010, while offshore is 29% lower. In areas of clean and alternative energy, technologies advancement of new energy car, Liquified Natural Gas (LNG) heavy duty truck and vessel restructuring, clean oil products, integration of refining and chemical, diversified feedstock sources for making olefin, and high value-added chemical products are making obvious progress. Comprehensive localization rate of the newly constructed, third generation of nuclear power unit approaches 85%. Technology research and development of the fourth generation of nuclear power generation such as small, fast, high temperature gas cooled reactors is under test use. In the area of clean coal utilization, technologies of desulfurization and denitration, high efficiency electrostatic precipitation have been adopted on coal-fired power units, which leads to a sharp decrease in pollutant discharge. In the area of recycling and reuse, technologies of residual heat, pressure and gas recycling, as well as flue gas waste heat recovery have been widely applied in industrial departments like steel and iron, building materials, petrochemical, nonferrous metals and papermaking.

② Integration of New Generation of Information Technology and Energy Technology Has Been Accelerated and Speeding Up the Construction of a Multi-energy Complementary System

Development and integration of internet technology and the new generation of information technology continues to proceed. The value of information and data has been dug in depth. New energy technologies and the new generation of information technologies are continuously combined and integrated, 5G, internet of things, cloud computing, big data, artificial intelligence and blockchain technologies have been gradually used in sectors of coal, power generation, oil and gas, which leads to a material increase in the degree of intelligence among energy sectors. In the area of energy internet, innovation of operation model for electric vehicles has been constantly made, functions like charging monitoring module, mobile energy storage system and SaaS system, energy connectivity module, smart energy management module, O2O business development and vehicle-net interactive module have been added to charging operation management platform. Functions like charging APP have been complemented. Interconnection between charging facilities and integration of platforms have been promoted, which realize interconnection among physical interface, service information and settlement of transactions, and the charging points hosting operations. Electric car aggregating operation technologies and high-efficiency energy storage technologies have been utilized in smart home and smart community. Massive data of electric car charging and discharging, energy storage and residential consumption are gathered and utilized. Demand side response cloud platform based on electric car are constructed, which could facilitate residential energy consumption management, be synergized with power grid operation, and create use value of end-use front facilities like power battery.

Industry integration between energy and information technology is dawned. The barriers between different departments appear to be loose. Rapid development of digital energy and information technology, as well as the technology of synergized energy sources management platform facilitate breakthrough of "shaft" between different fields of coal, oil and gas, power generation, communication technology as well as automobile, with communication enterprises step into energy, energy enterprises march into communication. Industrial barriers gradually collapse. Energy enterprises accelerate their pace to become smarter and more digitalized. Information is shared between multiple industries. On the industrial level, various entities actively promote sharing economy. Explorations in technology innovation have been further deepened on the subjects of synergetic stations, synergetic towers, synergetic signs and posts, centralized management of information gathering for elcctric, water, gas meters, four networks-internet, TV, telecommunication and electric- integration, and cooperative of vehicles and internet. New models such as power generation be renewables, effective integration of natural gas and geothermal, interconnection between information and various energy infrastructures, and fully interaction between energy consumption and supply have appeared to be well promoted.

③ Technical Breakthroughs Forge Rapid Growth of Emerging Industries and New Commercial Models and New Business Forms Are Emerging

Technical breakthroughs that largely expand industrial chains have become hot spot of innovation and creation in the energy industry. New energy technologies, new materials and advanced manufacturing technologies have been integrated. Breakthroughs create new energy and relative demand. Solar power generation industrial chain grows rapidly over the course of the "13th Five-Year Plan", the installed capacity (totaled over 2 gigawatts, among which centralized solar capacity accounts for 60%, distributed solar capacity accounts for 40%) of which ranks number one for consecutive years. Capacity of off-grid power generation is over 2 gigawatts, accounting for one third of total distributed capacity. Self-charging sales model, self-charge rent model, sell car and rent battery model, plus charging and battery rent model have been brought into industrial chain of new energy vehicles, which mitigate conflict of interests among enterprises of car manufacturing, battery manufacturing, battering rental and operating, power generation and consumers. This leads rapid development of up, middle and downstream sectors. The leading role of new energy manufacture and relative industries has been emerging, which prompt export increase of equipment like solar and wind power generation equipment, as well as vehicles for many years, and facilitate transformation and upgrade of relative industries and promote economic growth.

New energy technologies support the innovation of commercial model. The new models prompt re-shape of the ecosystem of energy. New energy internet technologies are emerging. First batch of 55 "Internet Plus" smart energy model projects has been initiated. Those all strongly support the innovation of commercial model. The involvement of capital, equity and human resource markets have enhanced enthusiasm of all participating parties, which facilitating the integration of flows of energy, information, value and capital. Models of E-commerce for energy marketing, financialization for energy trading, marketization for investment are created. Integrated Energy Companies (IEC) which provide integrated solutions for clients will be prompted to form. The concept and business model of integrated energy service will break the traditional pattern where different energy will be planned, designed and operated separately, and strive to achieve synergies of "electricity-heat-cooling-gas-water" horizontally, and of "integrated operation" vertically. Innovations of technologies and commercial models such as off-grid power generation, distributed energy market transactions, demand response promote the realization of information interflow between producer, consumer, operator, transporter and regulator. Energy ecosystem formed thereby shifts the traditional situation where producer and consumer are strictly separated. Efficiency of the energy system is materially increased. A reformed energy ecosystem is emerging, which could mitigate imbalances between energy supply and demand and reduce structural waste, and therefore increase comprehensive efficiency for the whole society, as well as reduce operation cost of enterprises.

(4) Pushing forward Reform of Energy System and Relative Mechanisms and a Fledgling Modern Energy Governance System Is Emerging

① Positive Changes Arose with Regard to Monopoly Energy Market and Effective Market System Encouraging Competition Is gradually Built

The reform of energy system and relative mechanisms is stepping into deep waters. Top-level design and supporting policies have been launched. Over the course of the "13th Five-Year Plan", programmatic documents such as *Suggestions on further promoting power system reform*, *Instructions on reform of the oil and gas system*, *Guidelines on promoting institutional reform for equities of natural resources*, *Decisions on removal certain licensing requirements and delegation of permission authorities* have been published, which leads to further reform and open-up of the energy sector and improvement of energy market and regulatory system. A new market structure is preliminarily constructed, with sizable enterprises taking dominant position, numerous small and medium-sized entities participating as supplement. Monopoly in the oil and gas industry is collapsing. Within the energy sector, reform of state-owned companies and the mixed ownership reform is going deeper. Market activity is heating up. The pace of constructing an open, unified, orderly and high efficiency energy system is accelerating.

The reforms of electricity and oil and gas system are pushed forward orderly. The degree of marketization increases. Pilot reforms cover almost each sector within the industry, with comprehensive reform taking the lead, supplemented by other multiple trials. Transition to shareholding structure of power trading entities is proceeding orderly. Trial operation of spot electricity market is initiated. Mid-term and long-term electricity trading mechanisms are further improved. Volume traded by market transactions is enlarging. Trial has been made on trading by market transactions for off-grid power. The sixth batch of trials on incremental power distribution business has been commenced. Reform of electricity pricing is exerting with greater efforts. Reform within the oil and gas sectors has made positive progress. Comprehensive promotion covering the whole value chain is carried forward orderly. Upstream exploration market is opened up orderly. Rights transfer of exploration and development is fully promoted. Societal capitals are brought in from various sources. Establishing China Oil & Gas Pipeline Network Corporation, starting the process of separating marketing from transport, as well as opening up long-distance and provincial network transported oil and gas to third parties. In the area of urban gas and oil product sector, open-up is promoted further. More market entities are encouraged to enter into the market. Market structure becomes more diversified.

② **Commodity Attribute of Energy Sources Starts to Rediscovered and a System of Market Pricing Is Promoted to Be Established gradually**

Market pricing reform for energy sources is being restored more rapidly. A system of market pricing is preliminarily formed. Programmatic documents such as *Instructions on further promoting pricing mechanism reform*, *Instructions on improving socialism market economic system* have been published. According to general guideline of "control the midstream and open up the upstream and downstream", pricing mechanism reform for electricity, oil, natural gas and heating is carried forward steadily. More attentions are paid to the price affordability of people in difficulties and special organizations. Cross subsidies are steadily reduced. A market pricing mechanism is gradually formed, which aids the expansion of market participants' spectrum and encouraging market competition. Pricing mechanism is gradually shifting towards the direction of reasonably reflecting scarcity of the energy, and external cost including impact to the environment and climate. By introducing differential electricity and gas price and other differential policies and measures, the supply-side structural reform and air pollution prevention and control is effectively pushed forward.

Degree of openness for competitive segments is rising gradually. A market pricing mechanism is preliminarily formed. The electricity department is steadily deregulating planning of power generation and utilization. Direct dealing between scalable consumer and power supplier is encouraged. A market dealing approach dominated by middle and long-term transaction is preliminarily formed. Improvement of project tendering mechanism for renewable sector is persistently made. Convergence towards accessing to the grid with comparable/ bidding price is ongoing. Oil and gas prices are linked to international market price. Dealing price is determined with reference to international market price. Wholesale and retail fuel prices remain under government guidance. However, market pricing process is aided by the price-cap policy. City-gate prices is primarily determined by transaction negotiation. Residential and industrial gas prices are converting to unified management. Direct supply gas, fertilizer gas, underground gas storage prices are deregulated. Meanwhile, natural gas trading centers in Shanghai and Chongqing have made valuable tryout on domestic oil and gas trading.

③ Reform of "Delegation, Regulation and Service" for the Energy Industry Has Made Positive Progress and Regulatory Mechanism and Legal System Construction Are Moving forward

Reform of "Delegation, Regulation and Service" for the energy industry is moving forward orderly. Government regulatory capability is strongly improved. Over 70% of the previous government approval items are removed or delegated to lower level. CBM mineral rights permission, as well as construction approval for oil refinery, LNG terminal and gas station are delegated to provincial or municipal levels. Power business licensing formalities "completed within one application". Separation of permits from business license" has been fully adopted in the Free Trade Zone. Index ranking of "Access to Electricity" is going up to 12. Energy regulation is further improved. Innovative energy regulatory policies which emphasis subsequent monitor as well as licensing authority delegation to lower level governments have been successively introduced. The policies define key tasks, standards, procedures and measures of regulation during and post operation. Regulatory system of credit supervision, "Internet plus supervision", "Random object, random inspector and result publication" which have been carried out on over 85% of the regulation items is further improved.

Construction of energy legislation is steadily promoted. Capability of regulating by law is enhanced. The *Energy Law (draft)* is under public consultation. The *Coal Law* and *The Electricity Law* have finished revision. Revision of the *Law on Protection of Oil and Gas Pipelines* is started. The State Council published *Instructions on harmonious and stable development of the gas industry*, Multi-ministries jointly released *Instructions on prompting healthy development of non-hydro renewable power generation*, which provide effective support for sustainable development of clean energy. Policies like *Regulatory measures for fair and open use of oil and gas pipelines* have been introduced, which improves regulatory mechanisms for power grid and oil and gas pipelines. Capability of regulating by law is further enhanced. Inspection for enforcement of the *Renewable Law* is conducted. Population of industrial laws is carried out into further depth. Monitor, coordinate and social involvement systems are established and improved. Projects approval, fund using and decision-making process of administrative punishment items are further regulated. Administrative review and litigation flows are further smoothed.

(5) International Energy Cooperation Is Carried forward and Security for National Energy Safety Is markedly Enhanced

① Deeper Involvement in Global Energy Governance and International Energy Cooperation of Multilateral and Bilateral Is Carried forward

China has actively facilitating progress of global energy governance. Voice on international energy affairs has been enlarged. China has participated in formulation of more than 30 multilateral cooperation mechanisms. Close cooperation is exerted with multilateral organizations like International Energy Agency (IEA), International Energy Forum (IEF) and International Energy Charter (IEC). China has become an allied country within IEA. G20 Working Group meeting on Energy Transition, and meeting of energy ministers are successfully held in China. We have also promoted foundation of Shanghai Cooperation Organization energy club. Other important international events, like China-Russia Energy Business Forum, APEC Energy Ministers Meeting, International Forum on Energy Transition are successfully held. We have also actively participated in organization and management of International Gas Union (IGU). Also, we have participated important international multilateral meetings annually, such as the World Economic Forum, Berlin Energy Transition Dialogue, World Energy Conference, Asian Energy ministers Roundtable Meeting, International Renewable Energy Conference, "Association of Southeast Asian Nations Plus three", which is also known as East Asia Summit Meeting of Energy Ministers, BRICS Energy Ministers Meeting, etc.

Bilateral cooperation is broadly taken. We have actively participated in the construction of a more orderly and more inclusive world energy governance system. More than 50 cooperating mechanisms have been set up.

Dialogue mechanism between China and EU, China-EU energy cooperation platform and high-level dialogue mechanism between China and OPEC have been created. China-Pakistan Economic Corridor Energy Working Group Meeting, China-Switzerland and China-Sweden Energy Working Group Meetings are held regularly. Bilateral energy cooperation is constantly promoted. Overseas energy supply is actively managed. Cooperation on nuclear with UK, Turkey, Bulgaria and Argentina is pragmatically prompted. Energy cooperation with Saudi Arabia is under negotiation. Progress on cooperation has been made with China-Pakistan Economic Corridor, the UAE, Brazil, Iraq, Myanmar, etc.

② High-level Openness Pattern Is Emerging and Diversity of Energy Import Sources Is gradually Improving

High-level free investment policies support is introduced, which promotes fairness and attractiveness of investment environment. During the "13th Five-Year Plan" period political and economic environment is becoming more complicating. China is determined to push forward opening-up and support globalization and free trade, and keeps opening up to the world. A series of policies regarding the foreign investment access system is revised, leading the open-up converted from the type of commodity and factor flow towards systematic open-up. Laws of foreign capital management are revised since 2016. "Three laws on foreign investment" and articles regarding investment approval in "The law of Taiwan compatriots' investment protection" are deleted. An administration model centered on Negative List is promoted nationwide. *Foreign Investment Law* is published in 2019, which clearly shows that a management system based on Pre-establishment National Treatment and Negative List is fully implemented. *Foreign Investment Law* is officially coming into force in 2020. *Special Management (Negative List) for Foreign Investment* revised in 2017 loose up restrictions of access in the energy sector, in which the stipulation of "foreign investment in oil and gas exploration and development has to be conducted through incorporated or unincorporated joint venture" is removed.

Diversity of energy import sources is improving constantly. Security of energy supply continues to be enhanced under the background of further open-up. Policies of energy import insist on the principle of multi-sources, onshore and offshore and balanced development. During the "13th Five-Year Plan" the Northwest, Northeast, Southwest and Marine Oil and Gas Passages are further developed. A pattern of inland import interacts with import by sea. Import from the east combined with west is gradually formed. At the year end of 2019, the north section of the East China-Russia pipeline is put into operation, which strongly supports gas supply to the Northeastern, North and even Eastern China. This marked the completion of establishment of the four energy import passages. Meanwhile, the first stage China-US trading agreement has reached a draft accord. Energy trading, including LNG will further increase the degree of diversification of gas import.

③ International Energy Cooperation Is Making Progress and Consultation, Contribution and Shared Benefits Principle Is Promoted in "Belt and Road" Countries

Four energy cooperation centers are built through strengthened cooperation between China and countries in Arab League, Association of Southeast Asian Nations (ASEAN), Africa and Central and Eastern Europe. *Agreement of Establishing China-Arab Clean Energy Training Center* is signed between China and the Arab League. China-Arab Clean Energy Training Center is jointly established in Beijing, where trainings of solar, photo-thermal, wind and smart power grids are held. China and ASEAN have built a neighborly cooperation and interaction mechanism, and have potential to be expected in cooperation in the area of clean energy trading and investment.

A Memorandum of Understanding of strengthening the cooperation between China and Africa is signed. In the spirit of "Belt and Road Initiative", flagship projects of "Jointly promote the infrastructure development plan in Africa" (PIDA) and *Agenda 2063* have made positive achievements. China has realized power grid interconnection and cross-border electricity trading with neighbor countries of Russia, Mongolia, Myanmar, etc. Four parties in three countries of China, Laos and Vietnam have signed MOU regarding ultra-high voltage power transmission. China has realized oil and gas pipelines interconnection with Russia, Turkmenistan, Kazakhstan, Uzbekistan and Myanmar.

Energy cooperation with "Belt and Road" countries is expanded. Partner relationship of energy cooperation is built. For the past 7 years since the "Belt and Road" Initiative proposed, over 40 multilateral and bilateral cooperation mechanisms are established, and over 100 energy cooperation agreements are signed. Cooperation within key areas continues to develop. Overseas oil and gas cooperation are expanding. Nuclear cooperation projects, as a rising force, strongly facilitate connectivity of policy, infrastructure, trade, finance and people to people. Five major oil and gas cooperation zones are established. Construction of multiple hydropower stations, thermal power stations, nuclear power stations and power grids in countries within these zones are undertaken by Chinese companies, which leads "going out" of Chinese equipment, technology, technical standards and service. The relative low-cost renewable technologies, products, equipment and service are provided to international market, which effectively promote the global energy transition and green development of countries along "Belt and Road".

2. Opportunities and Challenges of China Energy Revolution

The global political and economic landscape has been profoundly adjusted since the COVID-19 crisis. The green recovery is being driven, which will accelerate the pace of green energy development. Staring from the "14th Five-Year Plan", a new pattern facilitated by domestic and international double circulation development, will be set out by China with the goal of carbon neutral achievement. It makes the green energy transition particularly urgent. China energy revolution faces both enormous challenges and significant opportunities due to the mutation of domestic and foreign surrounding. New patterns of energy consumption and industrial types are emerging, pushing forward the revolution in energy consumption. However, the overall growth of energy demand is slowing, and it is becoming more difficult and uncertain to further promote energy conservation and emissions reduction. Development of energy transported across regions and high-quality energy are expected to increase, bringing more opportunities to promote the revolution in energy supply. But the pressure on energy supply security is increasing, as well as interregional energy transport and synergy between supply and demand are facing greater challenges. Nonetheless, the deep integration between new energy and ICT technologies brings breakthrough opportunities for energy technology revolution. There is still a gap between energy technology and the requirements of green development, while key technologies are facing key constraints factors. By modernizing the country's governance system and capacity, together with pushing for deeper reforms will strengthen internal impetus to the revolution of energy system. The reform has entered a deep-water zone with the large market reform resistance. However, the greening of energy sector is accelerated after the epidemic, which offers broad prospects for China to enhance international energy cooperation in green. In contrast, the risk of post-COVID-19 instability has intensified, while difficulties remain in international energy cooperation.

(1) The Energy Consumption Revolution Faces the Opportunity and Challenge to Keep Up Energy Conservation and Emission Reduction

① The Consumption Way to Meet Energy Demand Is Being Innovated and Large-scale Application of Efficient and Green Energy Is Expected to Be Promising in the Future

The integration of energy utilization and modern information technology is accelerating, and the innovation of energy consumption pattern is expected to create huge demand. The collision and fusion between new generation of information and energy technologies will promote the rapid development of a green energy network. Smart energy network as the distribution platform, e-commerce as the trading platform, energy storage facilities, Internet of Things and smart energy facilities, together with services of carbon emission trade, Internet finance and other derivatives are combined into one. It will greatly break through the spatial limits of access to energy products and services, make the radical change possible for ecological carrier in the energy consumption system, and promote the emergence of new energy consumption pattern. Green power, refined oil, natural gas, thermal energy and other products along with customized services through point-to-point trade, real-time delivery and payments online will also promote the new energy supply and demand ecosystem, and continue to create green energy mix. Meanwhile, there is plenty of room to energy conservation by optimizing the system to improve energy efficiency substantially.

New patterns of green energy utilization will be widely applied, while the upgrading of energy consumption by the whole society may greatly expand the space for energy utilization. It will take measures in line with local conditions and actively promote the "coal to electricity, coal to gas heating reform" policy. "Coal to electricity" or "coal to gas" is gradually spread in the suburbs and rural areas beyond the thermal network coverage. Breakthroughs in clean utilization of coal, improved fuel economy of motor vehicles, and ultra-low emission of coal-fired power generating units will be accelerated. Circular economy, gas fired boilers and electric kilns are gradual popularized in the industrial field. In transport sector, new energy vehicles, electrified railways, green and smart transportation are emerging. In addition, green buildings, building photovoltaic integration, smart city and modular energy internet system with multi-energy complementary are spring up one by one in the buildings' field. Hence the transition and upgrading of energy consumption in the whole society can be expected.

② The Growth of Energy Demand Is Shifting from Industry to Buildings and Transport, with more Complex Load Characteristics and Diversified Regional Distribution

Since the reform and opening up, the industrial sector has been the main force of China's energy consumption for a long time. As the industrialization entered middle and late stage while the economy moving to high quality development, remarkable changes are taking place in terms of the final energy consumption. In recent years, the industrial sector has conscientiously implemented the policy of giving priority to economy, actively promoted the high-quality development of manufacturing, and improved the overall energy efficiency. The industry system are transiting to a green and low-carbon cycle, in order to achieve a steady decline of the final energy demand in the share of the industrial sector, but rises continuously in the buildings and transport. Beyond that, the structure of energy consumption was improved. The main increase on final energy consumption is gradually shifting from industry to buildings and transport. On the contrary, the latter ones are more diverse with more decentralized and flexible load characteristics. Higher energy quality, transport and distribution, and timely connection between time and space are required, making it increasingly difficult to efficiently meet the needs of diversified energy demand.

In the future, acceleration of urbanization and population attracted by more central cities, will increase the demand for energy and significant complexity. According to the experience of developed countries, when the urbanization rate accounts for 30%-70%, it can be identified as rapid urbanization developing period. In 2019, the proportion of permanent urban residents in China reached 60.6%, and the urbanization pace will continue to rise rapidly in the next 5-10 years. With the improvement of the spatial pattern of economic and social development, continuous progress has been made in a new type of urbanization, labor transfer and equal access to basic public services, and it will vigorously promote inclusive development. When the population and economy concentrate in the eastern coastal areas, they are expected to gradually converge to regional central cities. It might bring increasingly final energy needs, and make the regional distribution of demand more extensive. Moreover, the multi-tiered, multi-agent, diversified energy demand as well as the need for universal access to clean, low-carbon, safe and efficient energy services for all will be fulfilled. That makes regional energy distribution diversified, and energy demand more diverse and increasingly sophisticated. That adds a source of uncertainty for the trend of final energy demand.

③ The Consumption Culture of Energy Conservation Has yet to Be Formed, and Effective Incentives Are still Some Way Off

The buildings and transport have gradually become major terminal

consumption, and diversifying energy use has yet to be formed a consumption culture to meet reasonable demands. As per capita living standards rise, the share of energy consumption in the buildings and transport improve sustainably. A large number of heating, electrical appliances, cooking, air conditioning and other energy-using services in residential life, public facilities and commercial buildings, mainly used the electricity, natural gas and coal. Passenger transportation and e-commerce hasten rapid expansion of trucks, railway, aviation and marine, on which mainly consuming refined oil, electricity and natural gas. The major consumption are fragmented, with diverse demand to energy patterns and consumers. The use of energy in accordance with reasonable needs will depend more on consumers' own conservation consciousness. Nonetheless, the social and cultural surrounding that supports rational energy consumption and restrains unreasonable way has not yet taken shape.

At present, although residents and others have a certain sense of energy conservation, the social publicity and education around energy conservation and emission reduction still needs to be strengthened. Some consumers take the initiative to buy energy efficient products and set appropriate indoor heating or cooling temperature, but there is still a large gap to standardize the energy-using behavior for all the ones. Phenomenon of lighting and household appliances waste, frequent opening or always on standby of water heaters, discarding food and packaging and preference for medium - or large-capacity private cars still exist. On the whole, the consumption consciousness of a green alternative is still vague, and people has not yet formed a systematic habit of saving. The energy-efficient standards of products and services related to the living areas of residents have been gradually improved, but the publicity and education that are widely and deeply rooted in the whole society still need to be strengthened. It is difficult to promote the formation of energy conserving awareness and habits among individuals, families, schools, communities and offices, as well as a consumption and cultural atmosphere that is "Honored to conserve, shame to waste".

(2) To Promote the Revolution of Energy Supply Are Faced with the Opportunity and Challenge of acceleratingly Greening Energy Mix

① The New Strategy of Coordinated Regional Development Promotes the Green Transition on Energy Supply, Which Is Expected to Arouse the Ulterior Potential of Green Energy Development

China conducts regional distribution to follow the regional development strategy. There are potential opportunities for green energy transition in key regions. In recent years, the Chinese government has successively introduced national development strategies at the Beijing-Tianjin-Hebei Region, the Yangtze River Economic Belt, the Guangdong-Hong Kong-Macao Greater Bay Area, the Yangtze River Delta integration, the ecological environment protection with high-quality development in the Yellow River Basin, together with the construction of the Xiongan New Area and the Hainan Pilot Free Trade Zone. A new layout for regional development strategy has been constituted. The new strategy to coordinate regions development calls for paying high attention to regional ecological civilization construction and green transition. Regional capacity of green energy supply will be vigorously promoted, to further optimize energy mix. Among them, relative enrichment area, such as Southwest China, Northeast China and The Yellow River Basin, are likely to improve the integration matching degree of regional economic development, industrial development and energy exploitation. In contrast, the capacity of clean energy supply is expected to be strengthened in the Beijing-Tianjin-Hebei region, the Yangtze River Delta, Guangdong-Hong Kong-Macao region and other economically developed regions, where key projects that "localized supply" will orderly be deployed.

Speeding up the construction of regional central cities and city clusters has brought unique opportunities for the efficient and intelligent development of urban regional energy systems. The construction of city clusters in the Guangdong-Hong Kong-Macao Greater Bay Area, The Beijing-Tianjin-Hebei Region, the Yangtze River Delta, Chengdu-Chongqing Region, the middle Reaches of the Yangtze River, and the Central Plains is expected to accelerate. These urban agglomerations and central cities include a large number of residential districts, commercial districts, industrial districts, public facilities and service areas, with quite distinct energy load characteristics and various demands. According to high quality development requirements, a clean, low-carbon, smart and efficient urban regional energy system needs to be built. Specifically speaking, it takes steps to construct urban energy cell body with standard functions, with economic energy supply as the goal to confirm the minimum scale and service radius. The system should ensure the optimization of self-balance of energy supply and use in each urban functional area. After that, relying on Internet technology, urban energy cells will be integrated to form new urban energy supply system and pattern, green, intelligent, efficient and safe. The construction of regional central city clusters in China will also bring great potential to construct new urban energy supply system.

② The Energy Supply Is still Dominated by Fossil Fuels, while Developing Green Energy still Faces Many Difficulties to Accelerate

Fossil fuels are always playing a dominant role in energy supply, hard to dissolve overcapacity completely. In 2019, fossil fuels accounted for 81.2% of primary energy production, which was 8.4 percentage points down since 2010. Despite the decline, the fossil fuel industry has been plagued by overcapacity in recent years, with rising supply and nearly no change in dominance. Although cut the coal capacity totaled by 920 million tons from

2016 to 2019, it still has about 5 billion tons per year of total coal production capacity up to now, about 1 billion tons per year more than the annual production capacity to satisfy the needs effectively. Installed coal-fired power generating capacity has exceeded 1 billion kilowatts, but the average annual utilization hours are only about 4,300 hours, which are still gaps between the economic operation requirements of coal-fired power generation unit of 5,000-5,500 hours. Oil refining and petrochemical capacity has exceeded 900 million tons per year, while large and super-large projects are still rolled out, with the pressure of overcapacity getting more severe.

There are still some barriers on non-fossil fuels, and distributed energy system is also facing the problem of sustainable development. At present, the development of non-fossil fuel is generally smooth, but there are still many obstacles. The problem of "Abandoning water, wind and light" has been improved but not enough, and the development of hydroelectric and nuclear is not as good as expected. Hydroelectric development will be restricted more seriously by resettlement, ecological and environmental protection. The economic efficiency of power generation technology will be challenged. And most of the good economic and technological conditions of hydropower has been developed, the future development space is limited. Because of relatively high cost on the new units of advanced nuclear power, as well as the public acceptance on account of safety, nuclear is becoming rougher to keep steady development. As fiscal subsidies decline, wind and photovoltaic power generation industry are into the parity era as a whole, and the cost on high proportion of grid connection of distributed energy is constantly enhanced. Therefore, there is increasing pressure to be forced to accelerate the breakthrough of key technologies, further reduce the cost, improve investment and financing channels, adjust the electricity price mechanism and solve the problem of grid-connected consumption through multiple channels. Ill-defined peak load regulation mechanism, together with lacking of flexible power supply and unreasonable layout, make the drawback becoming more prominent. Regions distribution have been unable to keep up with requirements of high-quality energy development.

③ **The Imbalance between Regional Energy and Economic Development Remains Acute and the Construction of Energy Transport Corridors, Peak-shifting Reserves and other Infrastructure Is under Increasing Pressure**

The energy development in source-rich areas cannot match with the promotion of high-quality economic development. The energy and economy in developed areas cannot blossom in tandem for a long time. The spatial distribution of China's energy resource is not balanced. Source endowment with reverse distribution of energy supply and demand has not yet been coordinated with the requirements of high-quality national economic development. In some regions, traditionally rich in fossil fuel, the way of energy utilization is still extensive. In some source-rich provinces in Northwest China, North China and Northeast China, the capacity for energy conservation, emission reduction and technological innovation remains quite low. There is no fundamental change in these areas, where presents a traditional development mode mainly relying on high-pollution and energy-consuming industries to drive economic growth. Although the southwest region is rich in hydroelectric, natural gas and other sources, it has not formed the strengths of industrial clusters in the upstream, midstream and downstream of green energy. In the eastern and central provinces with more developed economy, energy supply mainly depends on external input. In particular, the balance between supply and demand of natural gas and non-fossil fuels remains tense for some time, and the long-term contradiction that is incompatible with the level of economic development has yet to be resolved.

Construction of energy transport corridors relatively lags behind, and the capacity of emergency peak-regulating reserve is insufficient. The demand scale of "From the West to the East, the North to the South" continues to increase. In addition, on account of the "Auto transported coal" restrictions issued by a number of provinces, existing cross-regional railway transport pressure will increase significantly in specific time. Layout of crude oil pipelines is basically completed, but regional pathway of pipelines for refined oil product transmission and distribution are still inadequate. Furthermore, the overall density of natural gas pipelines is inferior, and the connectivity on key regions is an open question. As the Yangtze River Delta and other regions are increasing uniformly configured, there is a large-scale rapid development of renewables, electricity generation. However, centralized power supply cannot be matched well with distributed energy stations in regions. The contradiction starts to appear, stressfully on the overall security of the grid power generation. The energy emergency reserve system is behind schedule. Oil reserves have not yet reached the 90-day "baseline" recommended by the International Energy Agency. Respectively, with the minimum goal of 10%, 5% and 3 days share of annual gas supply, the capacity of gas storage and peak regulation have not yet been accomplished by supply or fuel enterprises and local governments. The peak load regulating capacity of power system is difficult to adapt to the requirement of large-scale grid-connected renewable energy consumption. The overall security problem of the power grid has yet to be solved.

(3) To Push forward the Revolution of Energy Technology, We Are Faced with the Challenge and Opportunity to Overcome Core Technologies jointly by Multi-party

① The Integration of the 5th Generation Mobile Communications (5G) and other Modern Technologies into the Field of Energy

Technology Is Accelerating and Breakthroughs in Core Technology and Key Equipment May Promote the Upgrading of Related Industries

The core technology system of 5G are facing to break through. In the future, the key energy information equipment market may have great development potential. 5G provides wide connection, high bandwidth and low delay information service on the basis of traditional connection, and adapts to various complex and abundant industrial application scenarios. It promotes the intelligent transformation for the full industry chain, including energy exploration, exploitation, transmission and distribution, processing and utilization. New forms of business, such as 5G Shared Base Station Solutions, smart grid inspection AI solution and transformer terminals based on open edge computing architecture, are likely to be achieved. With deep R&D of 5G core technologies and key equipment, as well as the gradual construction of 5G international standards and ecosystem, each step of the energy production, transmission and utilization will be further optimized. It may accelerate the digital transformation of the energy industry, change the way of energy producing and marketing, improve the efficiency gains and management level, and also create the added value of products in equipment manufacturing. The revenue of key energy information equipment manufacturing is likely to be higher than that of R&D and marketing services. More capital is attracted into the advanced energy equipment industry, and its future market share are expected to be greatly expanded.

Integrated energy solutions continue to be introduced, thus future energy development might be reshaped by new technologies and major equipment innovations. A new round of energy and industrial revolution, represented by new energy technologies, is on the rise. New technologies, tools, equipment and comprehensive energy solutions are constantly being launched, showing great development potential in different application scenarios.

Comprehensive energy solutions focus on smart energy production, storage, transition and distribution, consumption, and intelligent management and services. Existing technical barriers are attempted to break down, and a package of efficient coordinating response solutions are provided to terminal users. Among them, new disruptive technologies might be emerging in the fields of oil and gas, energy storage, advanced nuclear, new energy technologies, together with new power to build cars, charging piles and chips. They are expected to reshape the patterns of production, consumption and management of the energy system and lay a technological foundation for the further advancement of China's energy revolution.

② There Is still a Gap on Overall Green Energy Technology between China and the World-class Level and Innovation and Development Are Faced with Constraints of Key Technologies

The technical innovation pace of international green energy development is accelerating, while China's energy technologies in supporting green transition still have a way to go. International green energy technology innovation has entered a highly active stage. New energy technologies with greening as the main direction are iterating at an unprecedented speed. Major economies regard green energy technology innovation as a breakthrough point for a new round of scientific and technological, together with energy industry revolution. Also, it has become an important direction for green recovery after COVID-19. Technologies on unconventional oil and gas exploration and development in the United States took the lead in making breakthroughs, after that shale oil and gas have become a major source for increasing reserves and increasing production. Carbon capture use and storage (CCUS), which is expected to become one of the key technologies to deal with climate change, has been highly valued by developed countries. The United States, Japan and other countries have stepped up efforts on research and development. In comparison, there is still a huge gap between China and the world powers in energy science and technology, especially in the respects of the key technologies of deep shale gas exploitation, large-scale interconnection of high proportion renewables and greenhouse gas emission reduction. These key technologies are waiting for a comprehensive breakthrough. For example, CCUS technology can produce certain economic benefits by recycling carbon dioxide, which has the significance of popularization and application. However, due to the limitation of cost, there are still some problems to be solved for commercialization in China.

Key technologies restrict the transition and upgrading of the green energy industry, and it is still difficult to make major breakthroughs in independent innovation. In China, the comprehensive utilization of technologies and industries, such as electric vehicles, power batteries, shale oil and gas, hydrogen, energy storage and nuclear, has huge development potential. However, key technologies, the equipment and materials are all dependent on import at varying degrees, which impose restrictions on massive progress of the industry. Key technologies in deep shale oil and gas, deep-water oil and gas exploration and development, and heavy-duty gas turbine have been mainly introduced, digested and absorbed chronically. Serious bottlenecks still exist in key material of fuel cells, diaphragm of lithium batteries, sealing key equipment and other techniques. Limited by the deficiencies in basic theory, material production, precise instruments, high-end equipment manufacturing, scientific research system and other aspects, even though China has been working on these technologies for years, it is hard to make whole breakthroughs by relying on independent innovation in the short term. Furthermore, the mode of introduction then digestion, absorption and innovation on technologies abroad are faced with many challenges. New adjustment of international political relations, intensive intellectual property rights protection, export restrictions on key technologies, and poor commercial cooperation are all playing a part in this area. Key technology is still an important factor to effect China's energy technology revolution sustained for a long time.

③ **Multi-energy Integration and Interconnection Are Faced with Breakthroughs in Core Technology Thinking and Investment Gains of New Energy Technology Industries Remain to Be Improved**

It's hard to break through the traditional technology thinking of energy industry development. Effective elimination of barriers between different energy sectors is hard. Under the traditional development model, the energy sector has been divided into relatively independent subsystem and technology system with coal, oil, natural gas, renewables and other sectors as the core. Take coal-electricity/thermal supply system for example, after long-term construction, these centralized "point-line" supply and corollary equipment systems continuously strengthen the rigid connection between upstream and downstream internally and are relatively independent externally, thus forming an "energy shaft" over time. It is often set an extremely high percentage reserve for the "shaft" systems, with little choice for the downstream users. In the end, it leads a low overall efficiency of the system, making the bottom-up technology and innovation of business model little progress. Beyond that, the "energy shaft" also becomes a huge obstacle to the industrial transition and upgrading and adjustment of energy mix. Traditional ways of dividing the blocks of planned economy have been seriously unsuitable for the "integrated landscape, water, fire and storage" multi-energy complementary energy system, that cause channels of technical transformation, communication and cooperation to be impeded. However, the solidification effect of a large number of traditional energy systems will continue to exist.

For traditional state-owned energy enterprise, the technology innovation investment may be inefficient. It is difficult to get economic,

environmental and social profits from spreading and applying new energy technologies. In China, the overall level of energy science and technology cannot entirely meet the requirements of green energy industry transition and upgrading. The energy industry chain, value chain and technology system are not highly integrated and coordinated, which seriously restricts researching, developing and iteration of new energy technologies. Science and technology R&D investment from traditional state-owned enterprise energy is very large, but only research results can be assessed without thinking about the effect of promotion and application. That the economic benefit is not obvious. Through technological upgrading and rebuilding of China's coal-fired power unit in service, ultra-supercritical and other advanced power generation technologies are widely used in newly built large units, with an efficiency improvement. Ultra-low emission technologies for coal power generation, together with thermal combined electricity generation have become more popular. The superposition of pollutant emissions from large-scale units in the region results in excessive coal power pollution and total carbon emissions. The benefits between environmental governance and carbon neutral investment are not obvious. Renewable energy technologies such as photovoltaic, wind power and biomass energy have "dual benefits" of environmental pollution control and greenhouse gas emission reduction, but the external environmental benefits have not yet been fully internalized.

(4) To Promote the Revolution of the Energy System, We Are Faced with the Opportunities and Challenges to Deepen the Reforms on Electricity Power, Oil and Gas Systems

① Modernization of the Governance System and Governance Capacity in Construction will Promote a Revolution in the Energy System, and Offer Opportunities to basically Form the Pattern of

"Control the Midstream and Open Up the Upstream and Downstream"

Continuous progress in construction of modernization of China's governance system and capacity construction has continued, while theories for comprehensively deepening the revolution in the energy system have become more abundant. Major decisions and plans were set out to uphold and improve the socialist system with Chinese characteristics and promote the modernization of governance system and capabilities. Also, China has met a historic opportunity of further deepening the structural reform of the energy sector. *Several Opinions on Pushing Forward the Reform of Price Mechanism* issued in 2015 clearly stated that "we will push forward pricing reforms in water, oil, natural gas, electric power, transportation and other fields, liberalize prices in competitive links, and give full play to the role of the market in determining prices". In 2020, as *Building a More Perfect System and Mechanism of Market-based Allocation of Factors* and *Accelerating the Improvement of Socialist Market Economic System in the New Era* issued by China, we will further strengthen guidance on market-based allocation of factors of production and the construction of major market economic systems in society. It points out the direction for the modernization of the energy governance system and capacities, and provides a scientific guide for the continued revolution of the energy system. The pattern of "control the midstream and open up the upstream and downstream" is driven forcefully to be created.

The endogenous demand for energy system revolution is gradually increasing, and a modernized energy governance and regulation system is expected to be established. The revolution in the energy system will modernize the energy governance system and capacities, accelerate the transformation of government functions, stimulate the endogenous demand of the revolution, and shift the energy regulation mode based on planning and administration. The government should be combined organically with the market, by playing a decisive role on source allocation. Energy regulation will be put on a more prominent position. Focusing on strengthening weak links in regulation, playing the role of new technologies as "Internet Plus", Big Data, along with taking new ways to make the results of supervision known to the public, will promote innovation in ways and means of energy regulation. The establishment of mechanisms has been accelerated, while energy governance efficiency continuously improved. Moreover, the coordination and coherence of laws and regulations at all levels and departments have been strengthened, as the system of energy laws and regulations are likely to be further improved. The process of legislative amendment keeps to accelerate. Substantive breakthroughs may be made in the reforms of key areas and links, and the completion of the "multiple pillars"-the latest theoretical achievements of the energy governance system are expected to be quickly completed.

② Relatively, the Reform to Set Apart Transition from Distribution of Grid Power Generation Lags behind seriously, while Electric Power System Struggles in the Deep Water Zone

There is great resistance to the incremental distribution grid reform. Policies about competitive electricity sales are difficult to be implemented effectively. Since November 2016, nearly 500 incremental power distribution business reform pilot projects have been approved by the state in five batches, but no more than 10% of them have been built and actually operated. Some enterprise projects have been cancelled due to failure to meet the approval requirements. In projects under construction or in operation, the proportion of grid power generation enterprises holding or joint venture accounts for more than 80% share, but the participating degree of social capital is low. Pushing forward the incremental distribution network pilot project connected to the grid, power sale companies, customer service and other links faced with a variety of practical obstacles, basically in the state of stagnation or loss. At present, in the part of competitive power sale, the grid power generation enterprises in most areas of the country have established wholly-owned competitive power sale companies. But the asymmetric competition and contradiction between these companies and the ones with social capital are common. As grid power generation enterprises simultaneously include power transition, distribution and sales, the power sale companies may have related transactions with other sectors of grid power generation enterprises. To be in the advantageous position, it would affect the fair competition in the power sale-side market.

The construction of electric power spot market lags behind. The independence of trade institutions has obvious deficiencies. The spot market of electric power undertakes the function of discovering electric power price signals. By discovering complete electric power price signals, market players can be guided to carry out the medium-term and long-term trades of electric power, transmitting right and electricity futures. At present, Guangdong, Zhejiang, Sichuan and other provinces have issued pilot programs or carried out pilot power spot market construction to establish an active, secure and open power spot market. However, the construction target and development path of power spot market are not clear. Provincial power spot market is easy to form inter-provincial barriers, which is not conducive to the optimal allocation of resources in a wider range. At present, all the established power trade institutions are wholly sole proprietorship or holding by the grid power generation enterprises. Functions on the market trade committee are unclear or the role has not been given due play. Furthermore, the experience of pilot reform of power spot market in a few regions is not reproducible, and difficult to popularize.

③ The Operation Mechanism of China Oil & Gas Pipeline Network Has yet to Be Established and a Modern Oil and Gas Market

System Is quite Difficult to Construct

The difficulty of large-scale and efficient construction of pipeline network is increasing. A big problem for overall scheduling and management of pipelines and other infrastructure remains to be solved. The newly established China Oil & Gas Pipeline Network Corporation are faced with many problems carried from the past, so it is difficult to achieve efficient source allocation in a short time. The pressure load of the pipeline is relatively serious, as well as the damage caused by the third party is critical. Enormous transmission and distribution links, large cost, hard to recover investment for transmission and distribution enterprises exist. In the process of pipeline constructing, conflicts with urban and rural planning, ecological environment conservation and other sensitive aspects occurs from time to time. Construction of pipelines and storage facilities has become more difficult and it remains to be seen whether large-scale pipe networks and other infrastructure can be promoted in an efficient way. The operation and dispatching mechanism of oil and gas pipeline network needs to be further improved, the division of oil and gas guarantee and supply responsibility needs to be clarified, and the relationship with provincial pipeline network companies still needs to be sorted out and integrated. There is contradiction between the integration of pipeline network transportation and marketing beyond the province, as well as too many intermediate links in transmission and distribution. Also, the pricing and supervising mechanism of pipeline transportation fee needs to be improved urgently. There is still a lot of controversy about whether the gas operation license of urban gas pipeline is franchised. The separation reform of urban gas pipeline transportation business and sales business needs to be strengthened. In China, the spatial-temporal dislocation between wants and needs has greatly increased the complexity of oil and gas transmission, distribution and supply guarantees, so it should be enhanced for large-scale scheduling and management.

It is extremely hard to construct a unified open market system in the short and medium term, and the trade center are waiting to play its role effectively. In the next decade or so, oil and gas exploration and mining rights will be mainly controlled by major oil companies. The mining right transformation market needs to be established, while withdrawal of mining right needs to be strengthened urgently. In addition, the production technology service market to be improved, and the construction of the downstream market system to be strengthened. Cultivation of market entities, optimization of market structure, exploration of market trade patterns and others should also be firmly implemented. Afterwards, there are more need to be done, including of the construction of regional spot markets and the future markets of refined oil and natural gas. The oil and gas trade center is still at early stage of development, and the supporting mechanism such as trade service has not been perfected. The market environment of full competition has not yet been created, with few participants and inactive transactions. There is a phenomenon of "offline negotiation, online only for formalities". The product design of the trade center is not abundant enough, and the pipeline and storage capacity have not been included into the product design category. Hence various trade demands of the market cannot be fully meet.

(5) To Promote International Energy Cooperation Faces the Opportunity and Challenge of the Profound Adjustment of World Energy Pattern

① Tackling Climate Change Can Promote Global Energy Transition and Further Cooperation in Green Energy between China and other Countries Are Expected to Be Strengthened

Tackling climate change has become an important driving force for green energy transition, so the global energy green transition may

accelerate forward. COVID-19 crisis in 2020 delayed international climate change negotiations, but consensus on a green recovery is emerging among major economies. At present, countries are struggling to keep the epidemic under control and economic recovery, which causes great uncertainty in the global green transition. In the medium to long term, global action on tackling climate change will continue to advance under the guidance of the UN *2030 Agenda for Sustainable Development*. Green transition still represents the general trend and will be accelerated, which brings great potential for international energy cooperation. In the active support and guidance of governments around the world, the development of green energy can become an important focal point for global economic recovery. The European Union is firmly leading a way on global climate change, further cementing its "2050 net zero emissions" target, offering to do the best to "avoid past mistakes"—the stimulus package led to a rapid recovery in greenhouse gas emissions— and making each effort to promote green economic recovery.

China is always committed to optimizing the energy industrial structure and production layout, while green industries may become the most important part of Sino-foreign cooperation. During the "14th Five-Year Plan" period, China will maintain the strategic focus on ecological progress and set green development goals. The energy industrial structure and production layout will be further optimized, with the peaking of CO_2 by 2030 as the guide to promoted green energy transition. Meanwhile, China will actively promote the green development of "Belt and Road" and global supply chain, strengthen international cooperation in green industries, and strive to achieve green prosperity in the whole world, especially in regions. The green science and technology innovation will be taken as the driving wheel, green development and consumption as the wings, and the construction of clean and low-carbon, smart and efficient energy systems in key regions as the carrier, in order to promote a green energy production and consumption system that adapts to high-quality development. In China, the policy plan, advanced technology research and development, equipment manufacturing capacity building and market experience in promoting clean energy may have overflow effect—it will not only produce the expected effect, but also have an impact on people or society outside the organization. It is expected to effectively boost international cooperation on green and low-carbon energy.

② **The COVID-19 Caused a Global Economic Recession and a Restructuring of the International Energy Landscape and Intensive Risk of Instability in the Global Energy Market Caused more Problems to Energy Cooperation**

COVID-19 has exacerbated contradictions in the global energy market and activated a profound readjustment in the international energy landscape. In 2020, COVID-19 has plunged the world into the worst economic recession since the "Great Depression" of the 1930s, exacerbating the weakness of world oil demand growth. The oil price with the steepest decline in history and a wide range of shocks, endangered the energy, economic and financial security of many countries. The "shale revolution" has released to a great extent of the potential on oil and gas exploitation in the United States. In recent years, the dominance of the United States in the international oil market has been significantly enhanced and its energy independence strategy has been basically realized. The United States has become one of the major crude oil producers, becoming an important new variable for the world wants and needs imbalance. On the global oil supply-side pattern, Saudi Arabia, Russia and the United States are the "three pillars". Succeeded in achieving an "OPEC+" agreement to cut oil production without committing itself to a cut, its influence in the new energy geopolitics will move forward a further step in the future. The world economic growth forecast is uncertain, and the global energy market environment is unstable. In this context, the pattern of the international energy is undergoing profound adjustment, which poses great challenges to international energy cooperation. The stability of cooperation is what China has always struggled to find.

A new type of competition and cooperation among major powers in the field of global energy is being deeply reconstructed, results in difficulties in the future for effective global energy governance. In recent years, traditional security issues on geostrategy, superpower games and armament race have increasingly become significant in global affairs and international relations. The "super non-traditional security" puzzle on COVID-19 has added up to a dramatically increase of uncertainties about development of international relations. The epidemic has accelerated the realignment of major international forces, making global energy governance more complicated politically. Efforts to facilitate investment and trade in the energy sector have been affected by anti-globalization, and investment reviews based on national security objectives and discretionary powers have been strengthened to varying degrees. Here come unprecedented challenges in balancing the interests between producers and consumers, ensuring the security of the energy system, keeping uninterrupted flow of energy, maintaining the stability of the global energy market, and driving the sustainable and green recovery of the global economy. China is not only an important role in the new type of competitive and cooperative relations between major powers, but also undertaking the heavy task of consolidating and improving bilateral and multilateral energy cooperation mechanisms, and actively participating in the reform process of international institutions. Nevertheless, for China, there is still a large gap to participate in actual requirements in the approach, resource, experience and talent reserve. To effectively promote and lead the reform of the global energy governance system to truly acquire breakthroughs in global energy governance system, it still has a long way to go.

③ The Policy of Energy Institution-based Opening-up Has yet to Be Put into Practice and Multiple Pressures on the Normalization of Epidemic Prevention and Control, along with Economy High-quality Development, Have Raised the Bar of High-level Opening-up

Access conditions for foreign investment have been greatly relaxed in China. But changing from commodities and factors flow to rules, measures and other institutional openness is still an arduous task. We continue to improve the legalization, internationalization and facilitation and sound business environment for foreign investment in China these years. However, compared with other industries, the progress and degree of opening the energy sector are still relatively slow, and the actual results are not as good as expected. In the coming decade, the development of new energy technologies in the world and the pace of transformation are accelerating. Whether China can ensure energy security under the conditions of opening-up and lead a new round of green energy development lies in systematically upgrading laws, regulations, related to reform and opening up. In the energy sector, can we adjust the innovation policy, industrial policy and trade policy in the energy field and guide the change of international rules in participating in global energy governance? An institutional system that is open both internally and externally needs to be built and improved, based on the energy industrial negative list, to realize both active opening-up and effective supervision. It is also necessary to establish a modern energy regulatory system that adapts to the pattern of high-level opening-up.

Multiple pressures, including the normalization of epidemic prevention and control in China along with economy high-quality development, have made it more difficult to open up the energy sector as a high level. As the energy sector becomes more open, there are huge challenges in balancing development and security, enhancing local competitiveness, regulatory capacity and risk prevention capability. Facing the multiple pressures of normalizing epidemic prevention and control and high-quality economic development in China, achieving high-level energy openness is going to be insanely hard. On the one hand, the impact of the epidemic on the world economy will weaken the expectation of future energy demand, significantly reduce investment activities of energy enterprises. They will be more cautious in transnational energy investment decisions.In addition, the world economy will strive to achieve green recovery, caused traditional fossil energy investment greatly affected, and this has virtually raised the threshold of global energy cooperation. On the other hand, quarantine measures for epidemic prevention and control has affected the regular production activities and impeded normal international communications. The prevention and control of COVID-19 in countries around the world has become long-term and regular. Energy enterprises and institutions should take epidemic factors into consideration when conducting transnational and trans-regional business activities to reduce the intensity of association.

3. China Energy Revolution Outlook for the Next Decade (2021–2030)❶

China energy revolution is continuously deepened. A new chapter is opened for a high-quality development of the energy industry. Meanwhile, as the biggest energy consumer and producer in the world, China is taking effort in facilitating global energy green development. Looking ahead, China's energy consumption is continually upgrading. A new energy consumption pattern is gradually forming. Structure of the energy mix and sources is more reasonable. Peak-regulating reserve capacity is improving. Smart energy production system is gradually built. More independent innovations emerge, which leads the industrial transformation and upgrade. Systematic reform is going further. We are trying to restore the commodity attribute of energy. A fair, open, and orderly competitive market system is going to be built. International energy cooperation will be based on the principle of joint contribution, consultation and sharing benefits. Cooperation will be further expended. Global energy governance system is expected to be more reasonable. China will secure its national energy safety under an opened-up environment.

---

❶ Data from 2020 to 2030 on China's energy and others are based on the prediction results of the economy-energy-environment system analysis model, made by Institute for Resources and Environmental Policies, Development Research Center of the State Council. Relevant analysis results of China Electricity Council, China Coal Industry Association and other institutions, are also synthesized. The forecast model is built on the basis of computable general equilibrium (CGE) model, about national and provincial energy supply and demand balance together with carbon dioxide and the discharge of major pollutants prediction. According to the future economic development goal of high-quality and international experience and so on, it is used to measure indispensable energy demand, carbon dioxide and the main pollutant emissions of China.

(1) China Will Continue to Promote Energy Consumption Revolution and End-use Energy Demand Is Expected to Increase moderately, with Efficiency to Be Improved steadily, and New Integrated Consumption Pattern Is Going to Emerge

① Increase of China's Energy Consumption Is Expected to Slow down continuously until 2030 and Green House Gas Emission Will hopefully to Peak by 2030

A new development pattern of "Dual circulation" and a green energy system are to be orderly pushed forward, with the aim of reaching peak energy consumption by 2030, and realization of carbon neutral by 2060. There is an urgent need to promote China's economic revolution from both sides of supply and demand. From the demand side, domestic demand drive needs to be enhanced, and from the supply side, weakness and shortages need to be improved. Potential structural changes from supply and demand side will facilitate renewal of relationship between energy and economy developments over the course of the "14th Five-Year Plan". In that case, energy production and consumption will open a new chapter. By comprehensive estimation, overall trend will remain unchanged where energy consumption will increase slowly for a period of time. During the "14th Five-Year Plan" period, increase of primary energy consumption will fall slightly, with annual increase rate to be 2.5%. Average energy elasticity coefficient is roughly 0.43. By 2025, total energy consumption surpasses 5.5 billion tons standard coal with great effort to be taken, clean energy like non-fossil and natural gas will take a share of more than 30%. Oil demand is around 700 million tons, the share of which is 18%, share of coal falls below 50%. Energy quality is constantly increased. It is expected that by 2025, total society end-use energy demand will be around 4.5 billion tons standard coal. Total electricity consumption will be 9 trillion kilowatt-hours, with average annual increase rate of 3.5% over the course of the "14th Five-Year Plan". Electrification of end-use energy will increase 2 percentage points than 2020. Energy efficiency will be steadily increased. Energy used per unit of GDP falls 13% relative to 2020.

Development direction towards clean and low-carbon, smart and efficient, economic and safe is becoming clearer after 2025. Green House Gas emission will peak by then too. It is expected that increase rate of primary energy demand will slow down to roughly 1%. Energy consumption will not surpass 6 billion tons standard coal by 2030. Energy mix transition route of "less coal, more gas, oil stable and non-fossil development accelerates" is becoming clearer. Share of coal will decrease to 40%. Total share of gas and non-fossil will increase to 40% or above. Carbon dioxide emission peaks during 2025–2030. End-use energy consumption is expected to be around 4.6 billion tons standard coal, among which consumption by industry and transport is expected to peak in 2030. Building consumption, including commercial and residential, is still going up.

② Upgrade of Energy Consumption Continues and New Integrated Consumption Pattern Is Expected to Become more Mature

With transition of energy system towards Energy-Internet goes on, industrial and transport energy consumption pattern will convert from traditional single service type to multi service type. The industry sector is expected to break the energy "shaft". Comprehensive energy service is demanded which could flexibly satisfy various market entities in the entire industrial complex. High-efficient mode of electrification, cascade energy utilization and recycling will be formed. Consumption by transport will strive to become electrified, network-connected, intelligent, sharing and green. Integration will be carried on. Electric car, hydrogen energy will be put into broader utilization. Energy management from the demand side and market of demand response is starting to be formed. Construction of energy service market of peak load regulation, frequency modulation, voltage regulation, standby, surplus energy for sale is accelerated in order to meet disperse, punctiform and diversified consumer needs. Virtual economy is incorporated with real economy. A commercial model which uses the energy service network to discover and create higher added value is popularized. A more fair, efficient, sustainable, safer and human-oriented energy consumption pattern is going to be steadily built.

An "Electricity-gas-heat-cooling-water integrated" building energy service market is orderly constructed. A tailor-made energy consumption service model is gradually becoming mature. A new consumption pattern with size effect is emerging, which gathers and integrates various energy consumers and energy products and services by market forces. Integrated end-use energy service business with interaction between supply and demand is expanding. Transition towards comprehensive service from punctiform service. The integrated service is expected to include segments of consulting, planning, engineering and construction, maintenance and end-use service. Trans-sector integrated development and innovative general contracting form will be created which provides overall solutions. End-user infrastructure and integrated supply infrastructure will share coordinated planning and construction. Synergized energy sources supply and cascade utilization will be promoted, which satisfy the need of consumers for electricity, heat, cooling and gas. Complementary use of various energy sources will be realized, which provides diversified and flexible choices for consumers and meets energy demands comprehensively.

③ **Consumers Will Convert to Producing-consumers gradually and Consumers' Right of Choice Will Be Given Back**

Energy consumers are starting to convert. Producing-consumer is gradually participating in market activities. In traditional energy system dominated by fossil-fuels, producing, processing, storage, transport and consuming segments are distinctively separated. Consumer, as the end-user in the energy system, only played a single and unchanged part. With successive emergence of micro-energy system like distributed solar and wind power generation and micro-grid, more and more enterprises, public buildings and households, who use to be energy consumers is hopefully to become producing-consumers. Energy consumers could generate and reserve their own power, and might sell the excess power in electricity or comprehensive energy service market to other users, during which process producing, sale and consuming is integrated.

Energy market will become more developed, with consumer converted from energy taker to chooser. During the process of electricity and oil and gas system reform, consumers' awareness of choosing the energy type independently is gradually aroused. The relationship starts to transit towards a two-way selection one from the original one-way supply-demand one. Smart terminal facilities like intelligent meter is broadly used, by which consumers could understand their own energy consumption, share of consumption contributed by off-grid distributed power generation and charge and discharge condition of self-owned energy storage devices, and adjust consumption according to the conditions and market signals. With the maturity of peak regulation service like distributed energy storage, electric car and response from the demand side, consumers will realize identity switching, and reversely provide power to the system, which could be seen as auxiliary service provided to the power grid for peak regulation, and gradually become the active regulating force in the energy system.

(2) Energy Revolution Is Going to Be further Promoted and Green Energy Development Will Open a New Chapter, and a Multi-drive Energy Supply System Is gradually Forming

① Energy Mix Is Going to Be Improved and Green Energy Development Will Be Given Prioritization

Structural reform of the supply side will continue to be promoted. Share of clean and low-carbon green energy will be further increased in the energy mix. Energy supply is expected to be steadily increased. By 2030, total domestic primary energy supply is expected to be controlled within 5 billion tons standard coal. Share of supply of gas and non-fossil energy is hopefully to be increased to 45% or above. Oil and gas exploration will be further strengthened. By 2030, domestic annual oil production will be above 200 million tons. Domestic annual natural gas production is expected to be around 2.8 trillion cubic meters. Scalable hydro-power plants and small hydro power station modification will be promoted as a whole. Coastal nuclear projects are going to be developed efficiently and safely. Small nuclear reactor will be comprehensively utilized. Layout of wind power generation will be adjusted and improved. Both onshore and offshore wind power projects will be under developed. Solar power projects will be under diversified development. By 2030, the entire installed wind and solar power capacity will reach 1,000 gigawatts. De-carbonization of coal-fired units and phase-out of outdated units will be promoted. Efficiency of coal-fired units will be substantially increased. Ultra-low carbon emission transformation of coal-fired power plants will be completely finished, with ultra-low carbon emission coal-fired units taking 100% share. The emission standard is at advanced world level.

Improving and adjusting energy mix considering resource endowment and high-quality development of the economy. The main target of Eastern,

South and Central China is to secure supply of oil and gas, renewable and nuclear power. Development of distributed-energy resources will be given priority. While local resource is fully absorbed, excess green energy generated from other regions will be actively absorbed. The main target of Northwest and North China is to secure supply of fossil fuels and renewable. Sizable comprehensive energy complex which could secure the balance between supply and demand will be constructed. The main target of the North China is to secure supply of natural gas and renewable, as well as phase out the outdated coal capacity. The main target of the Southwest China is to secure the supply of gas and hydro-power. Construction of gas production base of trillions of capacities in Sichuan Basin, and Jinshajiang hydro-power plant will be actively promoted. Construction of alternative replacement production area in offshore region is accelerating. Comprehensive development and utilization of offshore oil and gas resources are steadily promoted. Layout of the refining industry continues to be improved. Resolving the problem of high-dependency on external supply of the Central and Southwest China will be given priority. Hydrogen will be developed in areas where preconditions are met.

② Constructions of Infrastructures of Energy Transport and Distribution Network Will Be Strengthened and Increase of Peak Regulation Storage Capacity Is Emphasized

Construction of peak regulation storage capacity will be strengthened. Security of energy supply safety will be increased. Construction of oil storage system is accelerating. Diversified oil storage manner will be promoted. We should increase oil storage seizing the opportunity of international oil price trough. By 2030 the scale of storage will be increased to 90 days above. Construction of gas storage will be strengthened. Construction of LNG infrastructures and infrastructures of peak regulation gas storage in coastal areas will be accelerated. Multi-level peak regulation gas storage system will be established. By 2030, gas storage capacity for peak regulation will be expected to reach 65 billion cubic meters, which occupies more than 12% of total gas consumption. Constructions of high-quality peak regulation power sources like main-reservoir hydropower stations, large scale pumped-storage power station, natural gas peak regulation power stations and electrochemistry power storage facilities are strengthened. Peak regulation flexibility transformations of co-generation power units and coal-fired power generation units are strengthened. By 2030, installed capacity of pumped-storage power station will approach around 140 gigawatts. Regional storage and merchantable coal emergency response capability will be enhanced. We are trying to reach a capacity of more than 15% of the annual coal consumption.

Establishment of energy passages will be promoted orderly. Resources allocation capacity will be substantially enhanced. Rail routes for coal transportation will be improved. Coastal supporting ports and wharfs will be constructed. Inland waterways will be improved. Cross-region coal transport capability will be enhanced. Annual railroad coal transport capacity is expected to reach 3.5 billion tons by 2030. Construction of cross-province oil and gas trunk lines and connectivity of regional pipeline will be strengthened. Intercity product lines construction will be accelerating. By 2030, total distance of crude and product pipelines is expected to be around 40,000 and 50,000 kilometres respectively. Total distance of natural gas pipelines will reach around 18,000 kilometres. Transport capacity of trunk lines will be over 5 trillion cubic meters. Meanwhile, flexible gas supply methods like LNG tank container multimodal transport, intermodal transportation and point to point supply will be promoted. Regional and provincial major grids will be further improved. The focus is to increase efficiency. Cross-province power transport capacity is expected to reach 500 gigawatts by 2030. Rural power grids will be fully and completely reformed and upgraded. Construction of power grids in remote and poverty regions will be accelerating, which aims to facilitate the service quality of power supply for rural areas.

③ Integration and Improvement of Energy Supply Will Be Made and Establishment of a Smart Energy Production System with Diversified Energy Sources Complementary Function Will Be Accelerating

Deep integration of energy production and information technology will be promoted. Intelligent development within energy production area will be accelerating. Broadly utilization of 5G and artificial intelligence technologies in energy production system will be promoted. The degree of intelligence of energy production system will be increased. By 2030, smart coal mining will be applied in main producing areas domestically. Material progress will be made with respect of "5G plus smart mine" construction. Intelligent oil and gas field construction will be promoted. Digitalized transformation and intelligent development will make great breakthrough. Digital oil and gas field construction will be completed by numerous oil producing enterprises. Digitalization coverage for producing oil and gas wells and plants and stations will reach 100%. Smart power plants construction will make substantial progress. Share of smart power plants of major power generation enterprises will be more than 60%. Widespread use of distributed power generation unites, like wind, solar and micro gas turbine will be promoted. Extensive application of new type small and micro energy power generation units will be further promoted. Green energy utilization is expected to realize to the utmost level. Gas distributed power generation will be developed vigorously. Deep integration and development of new energies like power generation by gas, wind, solar and biomass will be promoted.

Layout of network with synergized energy sources will be accelerating. Smart energy scheduling system construction will be vigorously promoted. By 2030, business environment of the electricity market is strived to reach top level in the world. Construction of intelligent oil and gas pipelines and smart power grids will make significant achievements. Construction of intelligent pipelines will be complete. Oil and gas resource scheduling will realize intellectualization and automation. Smart power grid will act as a pivot, which could facilitate realization of connectivity with multi type pipeline network like oil and gas pipelines and heat pipelines, coordination with energy storage units and power stations like chemical energy and compressed air storage units, demand response like charging orderly and V2G to new transport vehicles like electric cars and hydrogen fuel-cell cars, business model innovation cooperating with entities like virtual power plant and energy companies. Comprehensive energy system and Energy allocation improvement platform will be formed. Supplies of multiple energy forms will realize synergy and inter-transformation. Coordinated operation of centralized and distributed power source supplies will be achieved. Construction of smart energy scheduling system will be explored and promoted, which could integrate multiple energy sources like oil, coal, natural gas and power in the region and realize smart scheduling among them.

(3) Energy Revolution Will Be Promoted and Technology Innovation and Breakthrough Is Opening a New Chapter, and Key Equipment and Core Technology Is Expected to Realize Autonomous gradually

① **Major Scientific and Technological Projects Applications Will Be Given Strong Support and Promotion of Autonomous Design and Manufacture of Key Technology and Equipment Is Accelerating**

Adjustment and improvement will be made to the nation's innovation system. Technical breakthrough with respect to key technologies are trying to be realized by the opportunity of developing major scientific and

technological projects. By scientific planning, gathering forces, improving mechanisms, collaborative researching, and by developing national key research and major innovation projects which focus on most important contents within green energy strategy, we will strive to increase comprehensive competitiveness of the green energy technology and the industry. Promotion of China's National Science and Technology Major Projects will go further. New major scientific and technological projects will be initiated. Based on the principle of "Launch once matured", various projects are initiated in batches orderly. We are going to continue putting emphasis on "Core, High-end, Basic"-Core Electronic Devices, High-end Generic Chips and Basic Software- as well as other key technologies like power battery technology, key materials of fuel cell, offshore wind power, hydrogen production from renewable energy, and precise reconstruction of oil and gas reservoir. Feasibility of global public tendering for research and development projects of generic key technologies will be discussed, and the results could be published to all industrial enterprises, in order to stimulate the market vitality, and facilitate state owned, private and foreign enterprises jointly promoting technology breakthroughs.

Localization of research and development of core technologies and autonomous manufacture of key equipment is strived to be realized. Domestic energy technology promotion list is planned to be published. Alternative solution for risks caused by core technology is planning to be improved. Research and development of alternative solution for risks caused by core technology will be sponsored risk fund jointly established by central and regional government, finance institute, state owned enterprises and societal capital. Application of scientific and technological achievements will be accelerating. Numerous energy scientific and technological special projects are expected to be set up. Technology innovation could be promoted based on categorization of "Application and Promotion, Model Trial, and Research

Focus", hoping to resolve the problem of break and block points within the scientific and technical industrial chain. Domestic manufacture of core technical equipment will be promoted, which aims to transform technical advantages into industrial advantages. In areas where preconditions are met, advanced energy technology catalogue or list will be published and recommended, with government and state-owned companies' procurement giving equal treatment to imported technologies and equipment, and new technologies and equipment on the list. Promotion of localized and autonomous manufacture of technologies and equipment such as power battery system, power and electronics core equipment, heavy duty gas turbine, energy storage system, deep water oil and gas exploration and production platform will be accelerating, which might lead to broader utilization of domestic energy technologies.

② Advanced Chinese Applicable Standard Will Be Promoted and Establishment of a New Generation of Energy Technical Standard System Is Accelerating

Long term mechanism with the aim of resolving major issues of standardization is planning to be established. Technical standard within key areas and advantages in international competition will make significant progress. Synergy mechanism coordinating scientific research and technological development, standard setting and industrial synergy will be further improved. Organizing and working mechanism of Standardization will be further innovated. We will encourage International Standardization Organization to set up a branch within China. Challenges like construction of key technical standard system, development of core standard and whole value chain standardization performance improvement is determined to be tackled. Crucial core standard is planned to be published and implemented. Incorporation of major research achievements into national standardization project will be promoted. International communication and cooperation regarding standardization will be broadly carried forward. International standard cultivation trial will be implemented. Improvement of international competition advantages within green energy key technical area is expected to make substantial progress.

Development of core technical standard for emerging key technologies is mainly focused on. Trial application of the standard is accelerating. Layout of green energy core technology standardization is going to be strengthened, with focus on energy interconnection standard system, new energy transportation standard system, flexible direct current transmission and distribution standardization, LNG tank multimodal transport and integrated energy services and storage standardization. Hopefully it could expedite the achievements of numerous major scientific breakthroughs and core technical standardization. Trial application of technical standardization will be promoted. Trial application of standardization within the area of energy internet equipment and LNG tank "one tank to the end" will be established. Loop iteration of technical standardization system will be promoted, improved and developed. Standardization and Technology achievements which could be replicated and promoted are expected to be formed, which could lay the foundation for fostering international competitive advantages.

③ Innovation of Energy Technology, Business Model and Operation Format Will Be Carried on and Energy Technology and Relative Industries Will Be Fostered to Lead the Industrial Upgrading and Growth

Business model of energy Technology will be innovated. Inner innovation forces of micro markets are expected to be motivated. With development of energy trading platform, energy free trade is able to be implemented. New business models like virtual energy currency is planned to be promoted. Multiple entities in or out of the province will be encouraged to participate energy product trading. Development of mid to long term energy trading, time-of-use trading and ancillary service transactions will be pushed forward. Research and development of key technologies like multi-source data integration and value exploring will be carried forward, which aims to construct service and industrial systems of energy monitoring, regulation and scheduling. Energy technology innovation mechanism dominated by enterprises will be established and improved. Innovative service system for business incubation for small to medium sized enterprises in energy area will be improved. Enterprises' internal driving force of innovation will be motivated. An array of leading enterprises with international competitiveness for technology innovation will be fostered. Energy technology innovation assessing and incenting mechanism for state owned enterprise will be improved. The weight of innovation incentive in the operational assessment will be increased. Multi-level talent projects will be pushed forward deeper. With orientation of "high level, top-notch, cutting-edge and urgently needed", a high-level innovative scientific and technical talent group of China will be created. Research team and echelon will be formed. In order to raise innovation and entrepreneurial enthusiasm of core researchers, mechanism allowing them to take equity shares is introduced.

Construction of energy trading platform is encouraged. Multiple business models will facilitate the construction of new energy eco-system. Construction of an open and sharing eco-system in developed area based on characters of local energy producing, storage and marketing is encouraged. Taking "Comprehensive energy operation service in the complex" as an example, once comprehensive energy operation service platform is built, it could gather and integrate data from internal and external energy system network, support comprehensive energy operation service provided by multiple market entities, and realize energy synergy management, new energy and stored energy brought-in, demand-side response, flexible trade of multi-type energies energy internet data sharing. Another example is "industrial big data application comprehensive model", in which power generation, allocation, distribution and utilization will form smart interconnection and closed-loop linked operation. Smart energy industrial integrated application platform will be constructed on the basis of enterprises big data. Comprehensive data application model covering multiple areas will be explored. Involving numerous business models, an open and sharing energy eco-system will be more dynamic. The traditional organization and allocation approach of the energy system will be altered more deeply. Energy technology and relative industries will be the new driver for industry upgrade.

(4) Energy System Revolution Will Be Pushed forward and Price Reform Will Enter into Deepening Area, and Modernization of Energy Regulating System Will Be Promoted and fundamentally Realized

① A Modern Energy Market System will Be Created and Nationwide Power and Oil and Gas Spot and forward Trading Platform Construction Is Accelerating

Separation of natural monopolistic and competitive businesses is accelerating. A national energy market system that is fair, open and effectively competitive is planned to be constructed. The government will support and encourage more societal capital entering into the power industry, and continue the reform of incremental distribution business and electricity selling, with measures such as electricity consumption plan being developed orderly and more rapidly, and trading institutions independent and standardized operation being promoted. Establishment of power system operating mechanism with independent scheduling and power trading will be explored, which will realize effective separation of transmission and distribution businesses and assets. Power grids main business and auxiliary services separation will be implemented more deeply. Rules and mechanisms for renewables and distributed energy system to be connected to the power grid is planned to be established and improved. For resources like oil and gas, and coal, tendering for exploration and development will be completely implemented. Mineral rights will be acquired for value. Exit and transfer mechanism for mineral rights will continue to be strengthened. Oil and gas pipeline operation mechanism will be established and constantly improved. Operation of China Oil & Gas Pipeline Network Corporation will be carried forward steadily. Complete separation of transport and marketing for oil and gas pipelines will be accelerating. Fair Openness of oil and gas pipeline infrastructures will be realized.

Energy circulating market will be improved. A nationwide trading system of carbon emission rights for electricity, oil, natural gas, gas and carbon dioxide will be established orderly. The main focus is on development of electricity main and auxiliary service market. Electricity spot trading platform construction will be accelerating. Mechanisms and Rules of cross-regional electricity trading will be discussed and improved. Mineral rights for oil, natural gas and coal trading market will be promoted. Oil products, natural gas forward trading platform is planned to be established. Nationwide and regional oil and gas spot market will be built up steadily, and the operation will gradually be in line with international practice, which will be more attractive to more domestic and foreign investors. An oil and gas trading market with certain degree of international influence will be built. Research of establishing energy market and finance system inclusive of option and bilateral contracts, and mid to long term trading and spot trading is planned to be initiated.

② Pricing Mechanism of Energy Market Is Expected to Be Improved and Guiding Function of Fiscal and Tax Policies for High-quality Development of Energy Industry Will Be Strengthened

Pricing controls will be fully liberalized for competitive segments. A pricing mechanism dominated by market force will be formed. Government pricing will be mainly limited to public service sector and network natural monopoly sector. Pricing for natural monopoly sector will be checked and determined scientifically. Examination and supervision mechanism for transport and distribution cost of power grid and oil and gas pipeline will be improved based on the principle of "approved cost, plus reasonable profit". Electricity pricing mechanism will be further improved. Independent and incentive pricing system of power transmission and distribution based on performance will be established. Market mechanism for time-of-use pricing will be established and improved. Competitive segment of oil products and natural gas pricing will be liberalized completely. Relying on oil and gas trading center, pricing will be determined be bilateral negotiation or market competition. Energy cross subsidy will be gradually removed. Unification of residential electricity and gas prices and non-residential prices will be promoted more vigorously. Assistance mechanism for impoverished people and targeted subsidies for certain public service sectors will be set up and improved.

Guiding function of fiscal and tax policies for energy industry will be fully performed. Energy taxation which could reflect resource orientation and eco-environment benefit will be built and improved. Fiscal and taxation reform will be deepened, aiming to realize the integration of "domestic and international sources and markets" for regional energy supply, combination of "distant supply" with "domestic supply" and incorporation of centralized and distributed power supply. Energy taxation will be deepened, with environmental protection taxation being improved. Fiscal and taxation preferential policies with clear expectations will be constructed systemically. Broad application of unconventional oil and gas exploration and development technologies will be promoted. Special subsidy policies for deep water oil and gas, unconventional oil and gas exploration and exploitation, and the research and development of core technologies and equipment will be set up. Commercialization of core technologies and key equipment of hydrogen energy, micro nuclear heating and mining and rotary steering drilling will be promoted and accelerated.

③ Construction of Energy Legal and Regulating System Will Be Strengthened and Highly Efficient Energy Regulation System Will Be Built

Reform of "Delegation, Regulation and Service" will continue to go further, aiming to create a high-efficiency energy management and regulation system. Administrative approval process will continue to be improved. Approval process will be standardized and simplified. Administrative approvals will continue to be removed, or delegated to lower level government. Effective energy regulation system should be built. Reform of "Separating administration and regulation" will be promoted. An independent, unified and professional regulation organization will be explored to establish. Regulation measures will be innovated. Regulation with basic instrument of "Random object, random inspector and result publication" monitoring, based on credit-regulation, and complemented by giving special notice to major projects and entities will be improved. Construction of big data platform which could realize monitoring with "internet plus" technologies will be accelerating. Measures like punishment recording and media's supervision will also be used in order to enhance the authority and effectiveness of regulation. Measures like planning, policies and standardization will be jointly used to manage the development of the industry. Based on the demand of green energy industrial development and scientific and technical innovation, the consistency, uniformity, practicability and authority of national, regional and special energy planning will be strengthened. Policy system of green energy development will be established and improved.

Construction of energy legal system is steadily pushed forward. A modernized energy legal system is planned to be built. Revision of the *Energy Law* will be accelerating. *Energy Regulation Rules* will be discussed and made, which would set up or improve regulations, provisions, measures and approaches regarding energy industry regulation. With respect to *Rules on External Cooperation for Onshore Oil Exploitation*, *Rules on External Cooperation for Ocean Oil Exploitation* and *Natural Gas Scheduling Rules*, next step task is to introduce feasible and practicable detail rules for implementation. Policies for opening up sectors of oil and gas exploration, development, storage and transportation to domestic and foreign entities will be implemented. Laws on production and consumption, technical specification and standard system and the relative policy orientation of green energy will be gradually established and improved. Standard for renewable energy technologies and equipment will be set up and revised at an accelerating pace.

(5) International Energy Cooperation Will Be Pushed forward and with International Energy Governance Entering into a More Diversified Phase, Comprehensive Energy Cooperation Will Continue to Be Deepened

① We Will Participate in International Energy Governance and International Climate Governance more deeply, and Facilitate the Formation of International Energy Cooperation That Is more Pragmatic and Diversified

Comprehensive international energy cooperation will be enhanced, which could facilitate the establishment of a community with a shared future for the mankind. With a sense of historical responsibility of a major country and the great trust for securing China's high-quality development, we will further promote comprehensive international energy cooperation. Based on the principle of building a global community of shared future, the principle of different model for different countries, the principle of enterprise-led, being aligned to international practice, and the principle of mutually beneficial, and giving priority to efficiency, China will take energy cooperation as an entry point to build new type of mutually beneficial international partnership, and provide China solution for building a lasting peaceful, commonly secured, commonly prosperous, open and inclusive and clean and beautiful world. We have recently stated that China will increase national independent contribution, taking more powerful policies and measures, to let carbon dioxide emission peak by 2030, and try to achieve carbon neutral by 2060.

Global energy and climate governance will become more ever-changing in the post-pandemic world. China will pay more attention on enhancing the capability of participating in global energy and climate governance. COVID-19 has substantially changed main topics of Global affairs and international relationships. Multiple countries are under great pressure to balance current economy growth and the goals of employment with long term green development vision. However, most of the developed countries have basically reached consensus on green economic recovery. For the long term, green development is more likely to be the keynote and engines for global economy development. The world is going through challenging period of "Great changes in centuries" and "Pandemic in centuries". During this period, China's energy revolution will facilitate various countries realizing green economic recovery and tackling climate change. China is willing to participate in the adjustment of global energy and climate governance in the post-pandemic world. We are going to smooth the communication channels on multiple governmental and societal levels, and promote forming of a more reasonable and fair global energy and climate governance system.

② Comprehensive Open-up of the Energy Area Will Be Promoted

and Emphasis Will Be Put on the Realization of a Higher-level Systematic Openness

Openness of the energy sector will be more comprehensive and systematic. Emphasis will be put on deepening systematic openness. With the basis of gradual removal of foreign access limit, we will continue to promote comprehensive and high-level open-up of the energy sector, and try to create systematic and comprehensive new situation for energy cooperation. A Higher-level systematic openness of the energy sector is planned to be realized. Focuses of open-up will convert from segments of productive factors and capital access, to the whole operation segments. Taken the urban gas and thermal network system as an example, when the access limit for construction and operation is removed, governance capability will be greatly enhanced, with regulation becoming more efficient gradually. Share of foreign investment in China's energy industry is planned to be expanded. "Breaking" and "Making" will promoted simultaneously, in order to construct a set of market access rules and relative policies that are clear, transparent and open, which will be adjusted and improved during practice. International experience will be referenced, to further improve foreign investment dispute settlement mechanism. Foreign capital regulation system will be changed. A national security inspection system for foreign investments will be built.

The external and regional open-up policies will achieve convergence gradually, with differentials for different regions. In recent years, China's government has introduced a serious of major regional development strategies and regional open-up policies. Multiple regions will take advantages of policies like pilot free trade zones and key development and open pilot areas along the border to promote and realize regional energy high-level openness and high-quality development. For example, eastern coastal region has raised the proposal of whole value chain development of the oil and gas sector within its free trade zone. Government of Guangdong-Hong Kong-Macao Greater Bay Area are actively trying to create Shenzhen Natural Gas Trading Center, taking advantage of its highly developed financial industry. The western region are taking advantages of its geographical location neighboring to Central Asia oil and gas hosting countries to accelerate the construction of international oil and gas transport passages and diversified cooperation platform. Energy open-up is hopefully to present manifold new regional patterns.

③ Cooperation with "Belt and Road" Countries in the Area of New Energy and Oil and Gas Will Be further Strengthened and New Achievements of Energy International Cooperation Will Be Given more Attention

While interconnection of energy infrastructures is realized, a good foundation is formed for further strengthen the cooperation in new energy and oil and gas sectors. Interconnection of energy infrastructures will provide good foundation for the future. Cooperation spectrum is continuously expanded, cooperation quality is continuously enhanced, cooperation model is continuously innovated. International cooperation will convert from the current situation where fossil is taking a dominant position, to a new pattern where the new energy sector, like hydro, wind, solar, nuclear and hydrogen are all playing much important roles. The cooperation will also convert towards a higher level where export of "four in one"-energy equipment, technology, standard and service-will gradually take a lead position, from the current situation where the cooperation is dominant by products export. Meanwhile with regard to traditional oil and gas sector, we will meet the challenges of international market investment and cooperation environment together with "Belt and Road" countries. Major flagship cooperating projects will be carried forward steadily. International cooperation within high value-added refining sector, cooperation of deep water oil and gas exploration and development, and unconventional oil and gas will be further strengthened.

Regional cooperation will be based on projection of future global and regional political and economic patterns. We will try to make achievements of regional energy international cooperation. International relations and orders will undergo profound changes in the post-pandemic world. Regional economic and energy cooperation is hopefully becoming more important. China will adjust top-level design relative to energy international cooperation, and improve strategic planning and goal setting. Regional foreign cooperation strategy in the new era will be implemented. Multi-dimensional cooperation with neighboring countries will be strengthened. Over the course of the "14th Five-Year Plan" period, a new cooperation pattern of "1+2+3", where "1" represents the one pillar of energy international cooperation, "2" represents two wings of interconnection of infrastructure construction and trade and investment liberalization that could facilitate cooperation, and "3" represents three potential breakthroughs in the area of new energy, oil and gas, and electric car- is expected to be formed. Construction of cooperation community of energy international cooperation will be promoted gradually, aiming to secure national energy safety under the condition of opening-up.

Concluding Remarks

In the year of 2020, COVID-19 has made great impact and challenges to China's energy revolution and green transition. However, political determination, basic condition and supporting factors of China promoting the transition of energy sector towards clean and low-carbon, smart and highly efficient, and economic and safe direction remains unchanged. General principle of the energy industry to undergo stable and coordinated development remains unchanged. For some time to come, global supply will surplus demand, oil price will experience wide range fluctuation at a low level. Green transition of the energy sector will become more urgent. Domestic capability of reserve replacement and production enhancement will be improved significantly. Outlook for renewable development becomes brighter and clearer. Capability of securing energy safety will be improved further. System reform will go deeper, with industrial policies continue to be improved. New industries, new business models and new operation format continue to emerge due to influence of the pandemic, which provide vast potential for the high-quality development of the energy sector.

Standing at the meeting point of "The Two Centenary Goals", China will insist on promoting major tasks of the new energy strategy, ensure the implementation of decisions made by the nation and policies like "Six guarantee and Six Stabilities", accelerating energy revolution, improve the quality of energy economy, meet energy demand with reasonable supply arrangement, continue to improve the energy mix and promote the formation of new development pattern lead by domestic circulation and facilitated by domestic and international double circulation.

Progress Report of China Energy Revolution will be published biennially hereafter, aiming to set up a communication platform for promoting the great transformation of China's green energy industry and exploring the route of healthy, stable, coordinated and sustainable development. We would like to take this opportunity to express our gratitude to relative government departments, research institutes, universities and colleges, industrial associations, enterprises, international organizations, and numerous professionals who provide substantial support and assistance for the forming of this report.

Members on the editorial committee are all professionals with years of industrial experience, who have witnessed the origin and development of China's energy revolution. Consultants on the editorial board are all scientists of the energy area and academicians of the Chinese Academy of Sciences and Chinese Academy of Engineering who participated in the top-level design of the revolution and keep a hand in the promotion of the revolution. Special appreciation should be given to academicians listed below for their guidance and contributions made to this report (in the order of total surname strokes):

YU Junchong	MA Yongsheng	MAO Jingwen
DUO Ji	LIU He	DU Xiangwan
LI Yang	QIU Aici	ZOU Caineng
ZHANG Yuanhang	WU Qiang	LUO Qi
JIN Zhijun	ZHOU Xiaoxin	HAO Fang
HAO Jiming	HE Kebin	JIA Chengzao
GAO Deli	GUO Xusheng	CAO Yaofeng
KANG Hongpu	HAN Yingduo	XIE Heping

We would also like to express gratitude to the following persons who have provided constructive suggestions and comments, and their contribution made during the forming of this report (in the order of total surname strokes):

WANG Lei	WANG Jinzhao	WANG Fuping
SHI Dan	SHI Yunqing	BAI Yanfeng

ZHU Xingshan SUN Yaowei Li Wei
LI Yingfei QIU Jianhang HE Jinyue
ZOU Xiaoqin YING Guangwei ZHANG Yuqing
ZHANG Jianping ZHANG Daoyong ZHOU Juan
ZHAO Wei XU Jie GAO Yun
GAO Anrong TANG Yongxiang TANG Jinrong
HUANG Wenrui MEI Qi KANG Chongqing
ZENG Xingqiu